John Z. Goodrich

Exposition of the J. D. & M. Williams Fraud, and of its Settlement

The Chenery & Co. Fraud, and Removal of Timothy B. Dix, and Hon.

Samuel Hooper's

John Z. Goodrich

Exposition of the J. D. & M. Williams Fraud, and of its Settlement
The Chenery & Co. Fraud, and Removal of Timothy B. Dix, and Hon. Samuel Hooper's

ISBN/EAN: 9783337151652

Printed in Europe, USA, Canada, Australia, Japan

Cover: Foto ©Suzi / pixelio.de

More available books at **www.hansebooks.com**

TO THE PUBLIC.

That somebody, properly or improperly, has attempted to impress the public with the belief that I was guilty of gross official misconduct during the latter part of my term of office as Collector of this Port, scarcely any one, I suppose, is ignorant. The complaint against me began earlier in certain quarters, by denying that I had the "commercial experience" required for the proper performance of the duties of Collector. Representations like these were made at Washington as well as here, and so much credit had been given to them here, that it was said, about the time of my removal, even by those who accorded to me the "highest integrity," that "for the want of commercial experience (my) administration at the Custom House had been marked by *errors* which made (me) unpopular." That there had long been a growing unpopularity on my part with a certain class of importers and a certain public man, — though I could very easily have made myself their special favorite, — I know very well. I also know that I can point to all these so called "errors," and state precisely what they were. But whether they could have been "corrected" satisfactorily to the parties, by any amount of "commercial experience" without the aid of certain "mercantile usages" outside the range of commercial *integrity*, every reader will judge for himself. The class referred to quite too often confounded so called "errors," which resulted from the want of commercial integrity, with what they called "mercantile usage," and it was in that way, I think it will be found, that there came to be so many "marked" errors in my administration.

But at length the assault upon me assumed the form, either by insinuation, rumor, or direct charge, of gross official misconduct, and so much has been said to impeach not merely the *correctness*, but the *integrity* of my "administration at the Custom House," that I deem it my duty to myself and the public to submit such a statement as will present matters in their true light, which I now proceed to do.

SUSPICIONS AND RUMORS.

The following appeared in the Boston *Journal* of the 27th of November, as part of a despatch from its Washington correspondent "Perley":—

"Some of the officials of the Treasury Department here are anxious to know the result of certain investigations now being made at Boston into the distribution of a heavy penalty collected from an importer of French wines."

Mark the language of this despatch: "into the distribution of a heavy penalty *collected*." The implication is that the amount *collected* had not been properly distributed or *accounted* for, and that that was the reason the Department had ordered an investigation. Its officials spoke freely to newspaper correspondents of the investigation, and doubtless with the expectation that the matter would through them be brought to the notice of the Boston public. It may therefore be regarded as a semi-official despatch, which everybody understood to refer to the J. D. & M. Williams fraud ; to me as the accounting officer ; and to an investigation before the Grand Jury.

The Boston *Traveller* of the 1st of December, said on the same subject : —

" It is well known that a wealthy firm in this city, engaged in the wine and spirit business, was detected in defrauding the Government by false invoices. In order to settle the claims made upon it, the firm at different times paid $ 157,000, but of this sum the Government received only $ 127,000, leaving § 30,000 *to be accounted for.*

" Now the question is, what became of this sum? As the reputation of certain parties has been implicated, we understand the subject has been brought before the Grand Jury, with a view of having it legally investigated. It is alleged that the $ 30,000 was pocketed by *high officials.*"

Every merchant knows that if any money was paid in the settlement referred to, which *should* have been accounted for, but was *not*, it was paid to me as Collector, or with my knowledge and consent paid to somebody else. Of course I am, if not *the only* party, *a* party whose " reputation " is directly " implicated."

The Boston *Commonwealth* of the 2d December, says : —

" For some time past there have been rumors throughout the commercial community of this city to the effect that a considerable portion of a fine paid by a leading wine-importing house for a violation of the revenue laws *had not been accounted for;* and there have been grave suspicions whispered that the missing money had found its way into the hands of the late Collector, Hon. John Z. Goodrich, or some of his associates. * * This rumor in time found its way to Washington, and in some minds was associated with the recent change of incumbents in the responsible position of Collector. * * That Mr. Goodrich has been deeply injured by this rumor even in circles where it should be otherwise, we apprehend, from what we have heard, to be without doubt." The same paper further speaks of it as " the unfavorable rumor *so generally* associated with the name of Mr. Goodrich. * * The Grand Jury of this District is now giving it close attention."

Here the rumor or charge is that a considerable portion of a fine paid by a leading wine-importing house had not been accounted for, and that it was gravely suspected that the missing money had found its way into my pocket.

I do not understand any of these papers as intending to vouch for the truth of the statements they publish, but as merely repeating what had become common rumor. The charge had been made and repeated in conversations much earlier, and there would be no difficulty, if that were my present purpose, in tracing it to a responsible author. It found its way, according to one of the quoted extracts, to Washington, and was associated in some minds with the recent change in the office of Collector ; that is, that it was the cause of my removal. And it may not be improper for me to state, what I learned from two or three members of Congress, that in August, 1865, a short time before my removal, Hon. Samuel Hooper stated at an informal meeting of several members of the Massachusetts delegation, that he had received a letter from Mr. McCulloch, Secretary of the Treasury, informing him that a removal of the Collector had been decided on, and requested a recommendation by the delegation of another man for the office. The letter was not shown, it being, as Mr. Hooper stated, a private and confidential one to him. The other members advised, and some of them very strongly, against a removal, but Mr. Hooper said they had not been requested to express an opinion on that question, and added that Mr. Goodrich did not stand well at the Department, and, referring to the settlement of the J. D. & M. Williams fraud, said the Department thought there was something wrong about it. This was the idea conveyed. Other remarks were made by Mr. Hooper in reference to my connection with said settlement, which I do not here repeat. One of the delegation, as he informed me, made this reply : "This cannot be so. Mr. Goodrich has not taken money which he has not accounted for ; he is honest, and incapable of doing anything of the kind, and if it were otherwise, he is not such a fool as to take it in a case where it could be so easily found out." This I should not repeat, if it did not indicate so unmistakably the tenor of the statement to which it was a reply. This Williams matter was discussed at this conference, and it was understood, as some of the delegation informed me, to be a cause of removal. No other, as I understood them, was assigned.

The following are extracts from the testimony of Mr. Moses B. Williams, one of the firm of J. D. &. M. Williams : —

"A claim was made upon our firm during the year 1865 in behalf of the U. S. Government, for sums alleged to be due on account of previous importations of wine by our firm. There were two claims made, both of which were settled. Receipts were given by the Collector, or the Deputy Collector, to us for the money paid to the Government. The first receipt I cannot find, but the amount receipted for was $ 25,224, paid I think in the afternoon of March 28, 1865. The second receipt I here produce, dated May 8, 1865, for one hundred thousand dollars. We paid the money in the settlement of both the claims to Mr. Samuel A. Way. Mr. Way acted as our agent, and represented our firm in what he did. We paid Mr. Way not varying far from $ 157,000. We paid first $ 29,224, and got a receipt for $ 25,244. A portion of the $ 157,000 was paid between these dates — I mean the dates of the two receipts — and the balance at the time of settlement. We paid $ 7,000 to Mr. Way on the 2d of May, 1865. I did understand at the time said payments were made that $125,244 was all that was received by the Collector in settlement of said claims with the Government, and I have never made any statements to the contrary. It was not represented to me, nor did I understand that any portion of the excess over $125,244 was to be paid to Mr. Goodrich, the Collector. I am the member of the firm by whom said negotiations were conducted and settlements made. Not a particle of this money, not any money, so far as I understood, was paid to Mr. Way by us for his services in the matter.

"We had a correspondence with the Secretary of the Treasury in reference to the settlement of said claims. I should decline to produce it without the permission of the Secretary of the Treasury. (Adjourned for one day.) Having thought the matter over since yesterday, I have come to the conclusion to decline to produce the correspondence asked for. (On being told by the magistrate that it was his duty to produce it, adjourned again at request of Mr. Williams to enable him to consult counsel.) The date of the letter we received from the Secretary of the Treasury was the 5th of June, 1865. My answer was dated on the 12th of the same month. It was in the name of my firm. The correspondence was a confidential one, and I must still decline to produce it." (The matter was not pressed further.)

Extract of a letter from Mr. Samuel A. Way, dated December 19th, 1865 : —

" It is simple justice to Mr. Goodrich for me to say that I never paid him, or know of his being paid, one dollar, either directly or indirectly; and I am confident he never received from Messrs. Williams & Co., or any one else, any sum of money on account of settlement or anything connected therewith. " I write this without the knowledge of Mr. Goodrich or any of his friends."

Next I owe it to myself and the public to exhibit the

EVIDENCE OF THE FRAUD.

The history of the origin and practice of this great fraud upon the revenue of the United States, by a firm that has for so many decades taken first rank among the most respectable houses of Boston, will form an instructive, and in some sense an interesting chapter in the commercial annals of the country ; a chapter which I would willingly have allowed to remain unwritten, had not the Messrs. Williams themselves raised an issue which can be met in no other way. They have sought, and I believe still seek, — though convicted by their own tacit confession of their guilt, — to blind the eyes of a credulous public by the plausible pretext that they have been made the victims of persecution. It is not long since one of the largest capitalists in State Street remarked to me that he thought the treatment they had received from the Government was all wrong, as it would have been if the information he had derived from them direct, or through others, had been correct. And it was only a few weeks ago that Mr. Williams, senior, protested to one of the most intelligent and respectable merchants of Boston that they were innocent, and said he could convince him that they were, adding, that not they, but those who had taken their money, were in the wrong. They have taken great pains to create the impression that they paid a large sum in settlement, not because they had really defrauded the Government, but to avoid a long and vexatious lawsuit, which would have been especially annoying to the senior in the firm.

As a full and complete answer to all this, I invite public attention to the following facts, first premising that the information which led to the discovery and proof of the fraud, was furnished by Mr. W. B. Farwell, of San Francisco, who had been to France as the special agent of the Department. The proof was mainly derived from the books of the Messrs. Williams themselves, obtained by warrant from the District Judge on application from the Collector.

FACTS.

Prior to 1846, for several years Messrs. J. D. & M. Williams had regularly received from L. Roederer, the manufacturer, at Reims in France, shipments of champagne wine, familiarly known in Boston as the " Schreider brand." This wine was obtained by purchase from Roederer under a contract entered into in 1841. The price paid was $ 9 per dozen for quarts, and $ 10 for pints, deducting therefrom the costs of importation, such as freight, &c., and remitting the net amount so arrived at to Roederer on the receipt of each invoice or shipment.

In July, 1846, Congress enacted a new tariff which changed the duty on champagne from forty cents per gallon, specific, to forty per cent. *ad valorem*, which act took effect the following December. Prior to this, all the champagne thus imported by the Messrs. Williams was invoiced at $9 and $10, as the actual foreign market value. The duty being then specific, no reason existed for any other than the correct market value being named in the invoices.

From this date the story is best told from the letter books of the Messrs. Williams themselves. I quote from page 404 of letter book E. Under date of Boston, July 31st, 1846, they wrote Roederer as follows : —

"The proposed tariff bill, which we named in our last, has passed the Senate and will become a law, taking effect on and after December first next. The new duty on champagne wine is forty per cent. *ad valorem*, instead of the present specific duty of 40 cents per gallon, and 25 cents per dozen for bottles, which is about $1.15 to $1.25 per basket for whole bottles, and $1.40 to $1.50 for pint bottles, depending whether the dozen is estimated to contain 2¼ gals. or 2½ gals. Messrs. Piper & Co. have invoiced their wines at f. 2.50 (2½ francs) or f. 30 (30 francs) per basket on board, both for whole and half bottles, and have sent a consular certificate to that effect; if you should do the same the new duty would be forty per cent. on f. 30 (30 francs), say 12 francs, or about double the present duty. The law has passed the present week, and we havenot been able to see it. We will write to you again on the subject by the next steamer. . . . Your next shipment had better be accompanied by a consular certificate, you swearing to the invoice, *which is to be made at as low a rate as your conscience will allow.* That there may be a uniform course pursued by your houses at Reims, you had better consult with Piper & Co. and some of the other houses who ship much to this country, that there may be some uniform invoice price adopted by them on wine which is shipped here on their own account. *Your own discretion* will however tell you if this is advisable."

Again on the 15th of August, 1846, they wrote to Roederer, as appears by their letter book E, page 413, as follows : —

"The new tariff fixes the duty on all wines at forty per cent. ad valorem ; on bottles, corks, and baskets at thirty per cent. ad valorem. We hope that the order which we gave you on the 15th of July for twelve hundred and fifty baskets of wine, will be executed and arrive here previous to December 1st, at which date the new duties take effect. But, in order to be prepared for any accident, *you had better invoice this shipment at as low a rate as your conscience will allow you to swear to it,* because it must be accompanied by a consular certificate. We named in our last that Piper & Co. invoiced their wines at thirty francs per basket, on board at Havre. The principal houses at Reims had better adopt some system of invoicing; we mean those houses who ship much to New York and Boston, but you and Piper ship much more than any other houses. If you conclude to invoice the wine at thirty francs per basket on board, you must make the invoice in the following manner : —

" Invoice of ——— baskets of Champagne wine, shipped per ship ———, for account of myself, and consigned to John D. & M. Williams and Edward Codman & Co., for sale, or for their acceptance.

" C & W No. — to No. —, 1250 baskets Champagne wine, viz. : the wine at 23f. each; the bottles, corks, and baskets at 7f., 30 francs per basket on board at Havre. f. 37,500.

" The duties will then be cast on the wine valued at 23 francs, at forty per cent., and the bottles, corks, and baskets at 7 francs, thirty per cent."

Up to this time all wines received by Messrs. J. D. & M. Williams had been forwarded as regular purchases, as per invoices in the Custom House. From the form of invoice given in the last letter, it will be seen that to aid in covering up the fraud, Roederer was instructed to make his invoices as consignments, although, as shown, they were actually purchased.

On the 15th of September, 1846, they wrote to Roederer, as appears by their letter book E, page 431, as follows: —

"We hope that our last order for wine may be executed and forwarded immediately, so as to arrive before the first of December, when the new duties take effect.

"We shall soon be wanting more wine, and we would like to know if you can make any discount from the net amount which you *now* receive for the same quality of wine, after the *new tariff* takes effect. We ask this question because we are confident that we shall not be able to obtain an advance price equivalent to the increase of duty after December 1st, next·"

To this letter, under date of October 4th, 1846, Roederer responded as follows: —

*   *   *   *   *   *   *   *   *   *

"It is well understood that the accident of new duties falls to your charge, if unfortunately the ship should be retained and not arrive before the 1st of December next. This is in all justice and equity, and you have promised it in one of your last letters,

"Your question relative to a diminution of price is consequently answered in advance, and I refer again upon this subject to my former letters, viz.: that of 29th of August, &c. Since that letter, a vintage of excellent quality but of little product and of an exorbitantly dear price, has made it more impossible than ever for me to make the smallest concession, and I regret it infinitely, gentlemen, for I have always the liveliest desire to be agreeable to you, and to contribute as much as possible to the [greatest extension of my relations with your honorable house.

"But if you wish that I continue to send you that excellent quality that I have been in the habit of furnishing, and which still distinguishes my shipment of to-day, it is absolutely necessary that you add to the price of $9 for the bottles, and $10 for the half bottles, the augmentation of the duties of the new tariff, *and it will be necessary to take for a base the price named in the fictitious invoice which accompanies the wines*, that is to say, 35 francs per basket, on board at Havre."   *   *   *   *   *   *   *

Mr. Roederer being thus fixed in his prices, Messrs. Williams and Codman continued to receive the wine upon the old conditions, with the advantage of the reduced price in the false invoice for each shipment for use at the Custom House, At first Roederer decided that he could not put the price in the false invoice at 30 francs as they had requested, and proposed to make it 35 francs, but finally acceded to this request, and made up his false invoices for the Custom House at 30 francs, *which was* $5.58 *per basket, instead of* $9 *and* $10, *the price actually paid, less charges.*

In various other letters the Messrs. Williams instruct Roederer how to invoice his wine, and the latter responds as follows: —

"With this you will find the invoice of the 1567 baskets which are going to leave Havre the 20th inst. (   ) on board the Versailles. Have the kindness to credit me with this shipment for $14,570, payable as usual. M. Ludin — the shipping agent at Havre — will join to this letter (which will leave by the Versailles) an invoice legalized by the American consul; *a fictitious invoice which I have made according to your instructions*, and in accord with Messrs. Piper & Co., in French, as is their custom to do. I hope this will satisfy you in all respects."

This, however, did not quite satisfy the Messrs. Williams "*in all respects*," for under date of April 30th, 1847 (letter book F, page 44), they replied as follows: —

" The form of the invoice as directed in ours of the 31st of March, we believe to be the best that you can adopt until we find some reason to change it, *but we want you to swear to the invoice instead of Mr. Ludin.* You can swear to it before a magistrate in your own place, and the American consul must certify that due credit is to be given to such magistrate."

In a spirit of reciprocal accommodation·Mr. Roederer, from this time on up to the spring of 1865, complied with this request, and throughout 1847 he wrote, with every shipment, letters in which appear such expressions as these:—

Under date of January 6th, 1847 :—

"Here is the invoice, *and the fictitious invoice,* of the 1170 baskets. The genuine invoice amounts to $10,700, which you will please carry to my credit upon the old conditions."

Another letter :—

" To-day I have the pleasure to remit to you the invoice of the 483 baskets, which are going to leave the 15th inst. (July, 1847), on board the Wm. Goddard. Will you credit me with this shipment for $4,430, upon the ordinary conditions? *A fictitious invoice you will be provided with at the same time through Mr. Ludin.*"

Under date of October 11th, 1847 :—

" I have herewith the honor to send the invoice of ·the 527 baskets ordered the 14th of August, amounting to $4,850, and payable upon the ordinary conditions. *A fictitious invoice, conveniently legalized, you will receive through Mr. Ludin.*"

The Messrs. Williams, on the 14th of August, 1847, wrote Mr. Roederer (letter book F, page 102,) as follows :—

" We would like some wine, but should be glad to have it come direct to Boston. *We get along better with the Custom House here in Boston than in New York.* * * * Let the invoice and all the verifications be the same as those by the Versailles. You can make no improvement in these forms."

Again, later, they say :—

" We hope that you may be able to ship us some by the Moselle, particularly the half bottles, *which are passed by us in Boston at twenty cents per basket less than in New York.* There are also some other advantages in having the wine come directly into Boston."

On the subject of double invoices, the Messrs. Williams finally wrote Roederer on the 15th of November, 1847, as appears by their letter book·F, page 162, as follows :—

" *In your future shipments, we think it best that you should send only the invoice for the Custom House, and make no reference in your letters to any other price, but simply say in your letters that you inclose to us the invoice of the wine, with consular certificates, &c., shipped on your account according to existing agreement.*"

To this, Roederer responded as follows :—

" My next will remit to you the legalized invoice for the Custom House, and, following·your wishes, I will make no reference to any other invoice."

From that time to 1865, no other invoice than the fictitious one made for use at the Custom House, was sent. For nearly nineteen years the system of fraud thus inauguarated ran smoothly. Long

2

and successful habit had so sanctioned the practice, that doubtless it entered as much into the basis upon which business was done by this house, as any other element of its commercial ethics. It came down, literally, from father to son.

The following is an extract from the oath that was taken in each importation by one of the firm : —

"I ———— do solemnly and truly swear that the invoice now produced by me to the Collector, is the true and only invoice received; * * that I do not know or believe in the existence of any other invoice of the said goods, wares, and merchandise; that the entry now delivered to the Collector contains a just and true account of the said goods, wares, and merchandise, according to the said invoice; that nothing has been, on my part, nor to my knowledge on the part of any other person, concealed or suppressed, whereby the United States may be defrauded of *any part* of the duty lawfully due. * * And I do further solemnly swear, that to the best of my knowledge and belief, the invoice now produced by me exhibits the actual cost or fair market value at ———, of the said goods, wares, and merchandise."

SHERRY WINES.

This house also imported, and entered at fraudulent prices, the well known Sherry wines, as their books showed, and as they themselves confessed, by the prompt payment of $25,224, being the amount of three invoices, viz. : —

One October, 1863	$8,808
One January, 1864	4,156
One April, 1864	12,260
	$25,224

There were double invoices in each case — one for the Custom House and one to settle by. This was discovered very soon after entering upon an examination of their books. They requested an interview, and Mr. Williams, senior, Moses B. Williams, and Mr. Corey, met the Collector, Naval Officer, and others, at the Custom House after the close of business hours the 27th of March, 1865. Mr. Williams, senior's, first excuse was that they were consignees. But it soon appeared from answers to two or three questions, that they were purchasers, and paid no attention to the invoice price in making remittances for their wines. They then proposed to pay the amount of these invoices, and deposited the same afternoon United States 7 3-10 bonds sufficient to cover the amount, and redeemed them by paying the money on the opening of the Banks the next day, which was March 28th.

Most of the facts in regard to the Champagne were discovered after this, and a word more remains to be said on this head. Official investigations, set on foot within the previous two years, showed that Champagne wines were being imported at fraudulent prices. Seizures were made at San Francisco and New York. These alarmed Mr. Roederer, who, in a letter to the Messrs. Williams, under date of Reims, June 1, 1864, wrote to them as follows : —

"In remitting herewith a copy of my last letter, I believe that I ought to ask if the seizures which have been made in New York, of wines which the Custom House pretends are invoiced too low, renders necessary any change whatever in the prices in the invoices which I shall address to you in the future.

"If, according to custom, you address me an order for a shipment direct, —

which will probably take place about the first of July, — have the kindness to add your instructions upon this subject, for I desire that your interests shall be protected, and you know better than I under what circumstances the seizures in question have been made."

This elicited no reply ; and on the 21st of December, 1864, Roederer again wrote : —

"I had hoped to receive from you new instructions upon the subject of the value which it is necessary to indicate in my invoices for the wines which you order.

"The seizures which the Custom House has made render necessary the greatest precautions, and as the shipment is always made at *your risks and perils*, I cannot put the wines *en route* and make the invoices at the old price, for fear of exposing you to trouble."

To this the Messrs. Williams replied as follows : —

"It may be well to add two francs to the prices of each wines. * * * * We think *we* should have had no difficulty with *the old way of invoicing*, but as the other houses are troubled, and as they are all making their invoices higher, you had better make the change which we propose, as a matter of consistency with others."

Thus stood the matter when this long practised fraud was brought to light. The amount of Champagne wines alone, entered· at the Custom House between 1846 and 1865, by this old and wealthy house, at a fraudulent undervaluation, was over two million and two hundred thousand dollars, as shown by their own books.

THE SETTLEMENT.

Hon. Alpheus Hardy, at the request of Mr. Williams, senior, as he said, called at the Custom House to confer with me upon the subject of the alleged fraud, and the probable terms upon which it might be settled. Mr. Samuel A. Way had before offered, by authority, as he said, $100,000, which no one then proposed to entertain or even consider. Mr. Hardy was strongly impressed with a belief of Mr. Williams's innocence, from explanations he had made to him the previous evening. I presented the case and the correspondence to him very much as detailed above, and he reported to Mr. Williams, and saw me again two or three times on the subject. The sums named within which a settlement might possibly be made were $300,000 to $500,000, but I told him I had no authority to determine the amount. It was then supposed they were liable for the whole amount of the invoices, ascertained then to be about $1,500,000, but soon afterwards to exceed $2,200,000. About this time Mr. Hardy retired, and Mr.·Way again appeared as the friend of the Messrs. Williams, and was persistent and active in their behalf, and repeated the offer of $100,000. As I had no authority to settle or compromise, I deemed it my duty to present the question to the Secretary, and did so. Soon after Mr. Jordon, the Solicitor of the Treasury, visited Boston to advise in the matter. After laying before him all the facts, the question arose, what sum should be accepted of the Messrs. Williams in settlement. A conference on the subject was had between the Solicitor, Mr. Farwell, who had aided the Government in the investigation, Mr. Tuck, the Naval Officer, and myself. I stated in substance that I would not oppose a settlement, but my opinion was that a thorough examination before a court and jury would do more to prevent similar frauds, in the future, than any amount of money that could be obtained by compromise. Others thought it would be decidedly better for the Government to adjust the matter by compromise, but no one named less than $300,000. Finally, the sum of $350,000 was agreed upon as the lowest that should be offered in settlement. I concurred in a settlement on this basis, though I had favored a larger sum. The Solicitor then had an interview with the Messrs. Williams at their counting room, and offered to accept $350,000 and discharge the claim. The offer was declined. I was then authorized to compromise for that sum, and, if not paid, directed to report the case to the District Attorney for prosecution, and the Solicitor returned to Washington, supposing all the statutes of limitations had been repealed, and that the Williamses were liable for the whole amount of the importations back to 1846. The negotiation proceeded upon the idea that they were thus liable, — they offering $100,000, and the Government asking $350,000. At length it was discovered that by mistake one of the statutes of limitations had not been repealed, and that consequently there could be no claim on importations which had been made more than five years. The importations within five years amounted to about $550,000. The claim of the Government was thus reduced from over $2,200,000 to that sum. This I did not regard as a reason why it should be settled for less than the sum before named, viz., $350,000. But Mr. Farwell and Mr. Tuck thought otherwise, and favored a reduction at first to about $200,000 or $250,000. Mr. Way was untiring in his efforts to induce an acceptance of $100,000 in settlement, and at length Mr. Farwell and Mr. Tuck deemed it best to accept that sum, and proposed that Mr. F. should go to Washington and present to the Secretary and Solicitor the reasons which had induced them finally to favor a compromise for $100,000, and obtain the Secretary's authority to accept that sum if he should concur in their views. Prominent among these reasons were those given by Mr. Tuck in his published letter, viz., "I fully believed," to quote his own words, "though the facts showed a larger amount due, that the sums paid, being in the aggregate $125,224, were the maximum which the Government could recover, without protracted litigation, and without the delays and hazards to success which wealth and influence can always command." I did not give the weight to these views which they did, but was willing Mr. Farwell should present the whole case to the Secretary. He then prepared a paper addressed to the Secretary, designed for my signature, Mr. Tuck's, and his own, recommending a compromise for $100,000. This I declined to sign in the form of a recommendation, as I did not wish to express an opinion that it ought to be so settled, for my views were clear that it ought not to be ; but I was willing to concur in a reference of the matter to the Department, and to express my acquiescence in the proposition to accept $100,000 if it should deem a settlement on those terms advisable. Mr. Farwell then altered the paper so as to express substantially that idea, and I signed it. But on further reflection, and before Mr. Farwell had reached Washington, I decided to telegraph the Department and advise against the terms proposed, and did so, and then expressed very decidedly the same opinion by letter. On the morning of the 6th of May Mr. Farwell returned, and informed me that the Secretary had decided to accept the $100,000, and the next day the mail brought a letter from the Solicitor, of which the following is a copy : —

> "TREASURY DEPARTMENT, }
> "Solicitor's Office, May 6, 1865. }
>
> "Sir, — I have submitted to the Secretary of the Treasury the facts and papers relative to the frauds committed by J. D. & M. Williams and Edward Codman & Co., in the importation at Boston of wines and other merchandise for a series of years past, and the proposal of the parties implicated to pay the sum of one hundred thousand dollars, in satisfaction of all claims which the United States may have, for duties, fines, penalties, and forfeitures arising upon said importations or incurred by reason of the frauds therein, or other improper conduct in relation thereto, and the Secretary having examined the subject, directs me to instruct you to accept the compromise proposed. I have therefore to say that you are hereby authorized and directed to accept and receive from the parties in question, the sum of one hundred thousand dollars in United States legal tender notes, in full satisfaction and discharge of all claims of the United States arising out of the importations referred to, or out of the acts of any and all the parties interested therein, or in relation thereto; and that you will dispose of said sum according to law.
>
> "Very respectfully,·
>
> "EDWARD JORDON, Solicitor.
>
> "J. Z. GOODRICH, Esq., Collector of Customs, Boston."

I still hesitated, and on this, to me, very strong ground, viz., that it was not half the amount of the duties that had been unlawfully withheld, with the interest. During the progress of the negotiation, occupying some five weeks, Mr. Farwell, at my request, had computed the amount that the Messrs. Williams had saved in duties on the Champagne alone, and found that it was just about $150,000
Annual interest, for say nine and a half years, half the time, would be about $111,000 ; he called it   . . .   100,000

Showing that they had made and the Government had lost
at least $250,000
Mr. Way had also made a computation, and had frequently admitted that the amount of duties withheld was $100,000 ; he claimed that it would not exceed that, ... $100,000
Upon which the interest, computed in the same way, would
amount to about   74,000

                            $174,000

The average of the two sums was $212,000 ,
Mr. Way had also frequently admitted, when the Government asked $350,000, that as a matter of common honesty the Messrs. Williams should pay the amount they had actually saved and the Government had lost, and I determined to make an effort to secure at least this sum. Accordingly on Mr. Farwell's return I stated to him my determination to decline a settlement for less than the Williamses had actually made by the fraud, including the interest. I therefore, when Mr. Way called at the Custom House the next morning, presented the matter to him in this way: I stated that he had often admitted that as a matter of common honesty the Messrs. Williams should pay to the Government the amount it had actually lost · by their fraudulent undervaluation of the wines. He replied, "Yes, and I say so now." I then proposed that he and Mr. Farwell should

ascertain the amount of duty that had been withheld on all the importations since 1846, and offered to take the responsibility of discharging the claim upon the payment of that amount, whatever it might be, with the interest. His reply to this was that he and Mr. Farwell would not agree, and at once began to show him, or try to, that they could not. I answered that if they took up each importation and compared the amount in the entry and false invoice at the Custom House with the actual value and the amount actually remitted Mr. Roederer by the Messrs. Williams, as shown by their own books, — and it was all so shown, — I did not see how they could fail to come to substantially the same result. He responded, " We sha'n't agree, we sha'n't agree." I repeated that I did not see why, as it was simply a matter of computation ; that the loss to the Government in duties ascertained on one importation, would furnish the rule or rate on the aggregate amount, as the price paid was the same, and the undervaluation in the false invoices was the same through the whole period. " No," said Mr. Way, " we sha'n't agree upon the principle ; " and began again with great earnestness, I might almost say an excited or nervous earnestness, to point out to Mr. Farwell wherein they should differ, and added that Mr. Hardy would agree that his mode of ascertaining the amount of duties withheld was correct. " Very well," said I, " I am willing if you and Mr. Farwell cannot agree, that Mr. Hardy should decide which is right, and will settle upon the payment of the amount thus ascertained." Mr. Way, not liking this proposition, replied as before, " We sha'n't agree, I know we sha'n't, and there is no use in trying," continuing his efforts at the same time to convince Mr. Farwell that they should certainly differ. The discussion — at times quite earnest — run on in this way for a long time, Mr. Way admitting that the Messrs. Williams ought at least to restore all they had taken from the Government, but declining my proposition for no other reason than that he and Mr. Farwell and Mr. Hardy could not agree as to the amount. He finally said the sum would be less than $100,000. " Very well," said I, " then I will settle for less than $100,-000," and insisted that they ought at least to try, but he refused even to try. Whereupon I decided — and it was then my fixed purpose — that I would not receive the $100,000 and discharge the claim, and so stated to Mr. Way, who then retired, and, as I supposed, reported my decision and proposition to the Messrs. Williams. It should be stated that Mr. Way had learned the decision of the Department through Mr. Farwell before I had presented this proposition.

Mr. Tuck and Mr. Farwell disapproved decidedly of my action, and remonstrated with me earnestly against it, claiming that the letter of the Solicitor contained not only the authority of the Secretary, but his positive instructions, which it was my duty to carry out. I replied by repeating what I had before said in substance, that the $100,000 was not half the amount that had actually been made out of the Government by the fraud, and that a settlement for that sum would operate as a bounty and encouragement to fraud, rather than tend to check or prevent it. I insisted that while small offenders are held to the full penalties of the law, a great fraud like this, so deliberately and carefully contrived and entered upon, and so systematically and successfully practised for nineteen years, by parties who had evidently counted on their reputation and standing to lift them above suspicion, and thereby enable them to do unsuspected what otherwise they probably could not have done, — when pressed by Roederer to allow the price to be raised for their own safety, after seizures had been made in other places, it was with apparent reluctance they consented to an advance of two francs, adding, " We think *we should have had no difficulty with the old way of invoicing;* " — I say, I insisted that such a fraud, so successfully inaugurated and executed during so long a period by such parties, ought not to be so settled that the perpetrators of it could say that it had after all been a source of great profit to them. Rather than settle the case with such a result I much preferred to report it to the District Attorney in the usual way for judicial investigation and determination. This course, I think, and have ever thought, would have been the best for the Government. But Mr. Tuck and Mr. Farwell again urged their views upon me. They insisted that the matter had been referred to the Secretary *with the understanding that his decision should be accepted as final;* that it was my duty to comply with his instructions; that they believed it would be better for the Government in the end to settle in this way rather than take the hazards and delay of a prosecution, and I finally very reluctantly concluded that under the instructions of the Secretary and all the circumstances, it might be my duty to receive the $100,000 and discharge the claim, and did so. The following is a copy of the discharge : —

"Custom House, Boston,)
"Collector's Office, May 8, 1865.)

" $100,000.

" Received of J. D. & M. Williams and Edward Codman & Co., one hundred thousand dollars, in full satisfaction of all claims which the United States may have for duties, fines, penalties, and forfeitures arising out of the importation of Champagne wines and other merchandise up to this date, or incurred by reason of frauds therein, or other improper conduct in relation thereto, or out of the acts of any and all the parties therein interested. All books and papers of J. D. & M. Williams to be given up.

(Signed) J. Z. GOODRICH, Collector."

Let it not be supposed for a moment that it is any part of my purpose in the foregoing statement, to contrast what I did with what Mr. Tuck did. We differed very decidedly and widely in opinion, but I never had a particle of doubt of his incorruptible integrity as a man and officer. My sole purpose is to present as accurately as possible the part I took in the transaction, which I cannot do without referring to matters in regard to which we differed. Charged, as I have been, as the responsible officer in ferreting out this great fraud and settling with the perpetrators of it, with having received large sums of money which I have not accounted for, it is my right not only, but my duty to myself and friends, to state to the public precisely what I did. This I have done.*

---

* At the request of Mr. Tuck, to place him right before the public, upon a matter which, between us, was always right, I have consented to insert the following note from him : —

U. S. Hotel, April 19th, 1866.

Hon. J. Z. Goodrich :

Dear Sir, — I notice in reading my letter of the 19th of March, that my using the words, " by Mr. Goodrich or any one else," in that clause where I disclaim knowledge of the payment of an amount above a certain sum named,

THE SECRETARY'S CONFIDENTIAL CORRESPONDENCE WITH THE MESSRS. WILLIAMS.

Before the confidential letter of the Secretary to the Messrs. Williams, on the 5th of June, had he heard anything unfavorable to my conduct in this matter? If he had, from whom had he heard it? Mr. Hooper says *he had seen* my letters, — seen them at the Department, of course. I assume that this was before the Secretary's note to the Messrs. Williams; and that whatever he had heard unfavorable to me, if anything, he learned from Mr. Hooper.

If the Secretary had *not* learned anything unfavorable to me, is it not somewhat singular that he should have opened a confidential correspondence with the Messrs. Williams, who had been, as he knew, regularly and systematically defrauding the Government for nineteen years, without communicating at all with the Collector who had been doing all in his power to expose and stop the fraud? It is not usual to make confidants of merchants who have just been detected in gigantic frauds, rather than Collectors against whom there are no suspicions. But as the Secretary did not confer with me on the subject then, and has not at any time since, I infer that somebody had poisoned his mind. I cannot learn what he wrote the Messrs. Williams, nor what they wrote in reply. They say the correspondence related to the money paid in this settlement, but that it was confidential. It may be safely assumed that it contains something not in their testimony, as otherwise they would have produced it.

THE INVESTIGATION.

Why was it not ordered *before* instead of *after* my removal? The Secretary had been for three months before in confidential correspondence with the Messrs. Williams in regard to the " $32,000 unaccounted for." Immediately after removal he directs the District Attorney to inquire into the matter before the Grand Jury. But nothing was said to me about it. Why not? Was I suspected? Why, and upon what evidence? If not suspected, why has not the Secretary relieved me from suspicion long ago, instead of allowing it to be confirmed by what every now and then comes over the wires from his own Department? When the District Attorney called me I went before the Grand Jury and told how much money I had received

---

a casual reader might infer that I thought it possible a larger sum was received by you. I should accuse myself more severely for using language capable of such a construction, if the possible inference from the words used had not escaped your notice as well as my own, when I read my letter to you before publication. I had two objects in view in that clause of my letter, — one to make my denial entirely comprehensive; and the other to avoid trespassing upon your defence, officiously vindicating you, in Massachusetts, on your own ground, among your own friends, when I knew you were about attending to that matter yourself. Had I not known your means of defence and your purpose to use them, I should have made my assertions so broad as to have covered your acts as well as my own, touching the Williams settlement. I should have thought it proper, also, to have stated my own knowledge of your faithful course toward the Government on all occasions, and your incapability of any act unworthy of a most generous, patriotic, and honored citizen.

I am, with the greatest esteem,

Yours,   AMOS TUCK.

and what I had done with it. His report, not made a few days ago, will present the truth so far as he has been able to learn it. But it must go to the Department, and I have no reason from the past to suppose it will be furnished to me. I do not mean by this to complain of the Secretary. He doubtless has reasons quite satisfactory to himself for the course he has pursued.

THE THIRTY-TWO THOUSAND DOLLARS.

Moses B. Williams testifies that besides the $125,224 paid to the Government, $32,000 was paid to Mr. Way, but "not a particle" was to be paid to him as compensation for his services. Consequently it was all paid for the purpose of being used — it is not now pretended to the contrary, I suppose — wherever and with whomsoever it would accomplish most in promoting favorable dispositions and securing effective aid· and influence in moderating the demands of the Government. In other words, it was paid to "grease the wheels." I had not the slightest suspicion at the time that money was used, nor did it once occur to me that it could be had for any such purpose. And I take great pleasure in being able to say that I have no belief whatever that one cent of this $32,000 was paid to any officer connected with the Boston Custom House, including Mr. French, who was acting as Special Deputy in this and a few other cases which arose before he resigned as one of the regular Deputies, the first of April. I have the satisfaction of feeling that it was not deemed best to suggest to me that money could be had, if desired ; at any rate, the suggestion was not made. And I am very sure, if I had had the least suspicion that such means had been used to compass a settlement on easier terms, I should never have signed a receipt discharging the claim.

One word more in this connection. Assailed as I have been, wickedly and cruelly stabbed in the dark, as I have been, I may be allowed to affirm, as I do explicitly and positively, that I performed faithfully the onerous and responsible duty which was thrust upon me by the discovery of this fraud. Others might have performed it better, but no one could have tried harder to discharge his whole duty to the Government and the public, than I did to the extent of my ability and according to my best judgment.

3

CHENERY & CO. AND DIX CASE, AND MR. HOOPER'S REPORT.

It is due to the public, if not to myself, that I explain another gross fraud, and the means by which men high in military and civil position have sought to justify it and the parties to it at the Department. The Williams fraud was greater in amount, but the means employed were no worse. Let everyone read the following statement, and judge for himself : —

FACTS.

On the 24th of July, 1862, Messrs. Chenery & Co. imported a cargo of rum, sugar, and molasses, and on the same day made a warehouse entry of the whole cargo. The Inspector, who superintended the unlading, delivered it all to the Storekeeper for warehousing on the 25th, and took warehouse receipts. The following is a copy of the receipt for the sugar, excepting the marks and numbers : —

"Boston, July 25th, 1862. " Received *in warehouse* at C. H. B. [Custom House Block] from on board brig Wm. Moore, Klynn, Master, from St. Croix, twenty-four hhds. and six bbls. sugar, marked and numbered as in margin, and imported by Chenery & Co.

"Signed by the Storekeeper."

Another receipt in the same form was given for the molasses, and a third for the rum. The rum was immediately sent to United States Bonded Warehouse, but the sugar and molasses, at the request of Chenery & Co., was allowed to remain on the wharf, as they expected to sell it the next day, pay the duties and withdraw it, which' they did. It was, however, in the custody and control of the Government, represented by the Storekeeper, — who might at any moment have sent it to the store, — and was considered as constructively ware-housed, according to the well-known custom in such cases.

On the 26th, the Inspector made the usual return at the Custom House that the vessel had been discharged and the cargo " warehoused or stored on the 25th," and left with his return the Storekeeper's warehouse receipts.

On the same day the Storekeeper made his return, which was on the back of the order to receive the cargo into store, and was in these words : — " The merchandise permitted within was *received into store on the 25th day of July*, 1862."

On the same day also, July 26th, Chenery & Co. paid the duty on the sugar and molasses, having sold it as expected, and withdrew it " from warehouse," and received the usual order or permit to the Storekeeper to deliver it. This was Saturday, and it suited their convenience to hold the order till Monday, the 28th, when they presented it and received the goods. The Storekeeper then returned the order to the Custom House, and indorsed on it, " Delivered *out* July 28th, 1862."

The rum remained in bonded warehouse till the 28th of October.

which was three months and four days after it was imported. Chenery & Co. then applied to Mr. Payne, Warehouse Book-keeper, to withdraw it, who informed them that as more than three months had elapsed since it was imported, it was subject to double duty. To this they objected, and presented the question to Mr. Timothy B. Dix, principal Storage Clerk, who stated that as it appeared from the return of the Storekeeper that it had been in warehouse more three months, it could not be withdrawn without paying double duty, or an additional duty of fifty-nine cents a gallon. The time of *warehousing* was no otherwise important than the conclusive evidence it furnished that the rum had been *imported* more than three months, the law being that it was subject to double duty if not withdrawn within three months from importation. How to get over this evidence and that furnished by Chenery & Co.'s oath, made on the original entry, that it was imported on the 24th of July, was the question. They went to the warehouse and endeavored to persuade the Storekeeper that it was not warehoused till the 28th of July, and that his return was wrong. But the Storekeeper, after examining his books, was satisfied he received the rum into warehouse on the 25th of July, and that his return was right. They then requested him to go to the Custom House and confer with Payne and Dix, two old and experienced clerks, and see if it could not be arranged in some way, which he did. He first saw Payne, who went with him to Dix's desk. The Storekeeper stated to Dix and Payne that he received the rum, sugar, and molasses on the 25th of July, and delivered the sugar and molasses *out* to Chenery & Co. on the 28th, as his return showed. It has never been pretended that he made a different statement, always affirming the correctness of his returns. Mr. Dix then said that "upon the Storekeeper's *statement of the facts, in accordance with the usual practice the return should have been dated the 28th of July instead of the 26th, and that it would be proper to alter it.*" Finally, the Storekeeper, by the advice and direction of Mr. Dix, as Mr. Payne and the Storekeeper both say, altered his return, which was, as I have said, on the back of the order to receive into warehouse. As originally made it was as follows : —

" Boston, July 26th, 1862.
" The merchandise [which included the rum, sugar and molasses] permitted within, was received into store on the 25th day of July, 1862."

As altered, it was as follows : —

" Boston, July 28th, 1862.
" The merchandise permitted within was received into store on the 25th and 28th day of July, 1862."

The alteration consisted in inserting in the body of the return after the figures " 25 " the word and figures " and 28," and by making the figure " 6 " in the date into " 8," so that the date would be 28th instead of 26th. In this way the time of the deposit or warehousing of the rum, treating the whole as one transaction, and dating from the deposit of the sugar and molasses, *thus fixed by the altered return* at the 28th of July, was brought within three months from the 28th of October. But this was not enough, because, while the 28th of October might not be more than three months from the time of *deposit* in warehouse, it might be more than that from the time of *im-*

portation. It was therefore necessary, under the law existing at that time, to show that the withdrawal on the 28th of October would not exceed three months from *importation.* This was done by allowing Chenery & Co. to state in their withdrawal entry of the rum on the 28th of October, that it was imported on the 28th day of July; and they did so state, although in the original entry on the 24th of July, they had sworn, *as the fact was,* that it was imported on the 24th.

Upon this *altered* and *false* return of the Storekeeper, and their own *false* statement that the rum was imported on the 28th of July, Chenery & Co. were allowed to pay the single duty of fifty-nine cents a gallon and withdraw it, which they did. The additional duty was $2,993.66, and the whole purpose was to relieve them from the payment of this sum. There was no other conceivable motive or necessity for altering the return, or making the false statement as to the time of importation, and Chenery & Co. and Dix were obliged to admit, and did admit, that such was the purpose.

A letter from the Commissioner of Customs, dated the 20th of the following March (1863), inquiring why a duty of one hundred and eighteen cents instead of fifty-nine had not been collected on the rum, led to the disclosure of the foregoing facts, which was the first information I or either of my Deputies had on the subject. The rum still remained in warehouse on storage, and I immediately revoked the order to deliver, and gave directions to retain it till the additional duty of $2,993.64 was paid, and payment was made soon after. Mr. Dix was removed (Payne and the Storekeeper resigned), and his removal was approved by the Secretary upon a report of the facts, with copies of all the papers' relating to the case. His brother, General John A. Dix, soon after appealed to the Secretary to direct that he be reinstated, on the ground that injustice had been done him by the removal. The Secretary (Mr. Chase), though he did not claim the right to reinstate after having approved of the removal, was willing, as a friend to General Dix, to inquire again and thoroughly into the facts, and do what he properly might. With this view, he wrote to Mr. Hooper on the 28th of July, 1863, and inclosed all the papers which I had forwarded, and asked him to ascertain all the facts and report them with his opinion, and especially to report whether he agreed with the Collector. The forepart of August Mr. Hooper called on me at the Custom House, and showed me his letter from the Secretary. I at once made a full explanation of all the facts and the views I entertained, and showed him the Storekeeper's warehouse receipts, dated July 25th, the Inspector's return, dated the 26th, the entry of Chenery & Co., *withdrawing the sugar and molasses, on the 26th,* and the Storekeeper's *altered* return, and pointed out what the alteration was. I understood him to express opinions which agreed with my own ; he said nothing to indicate that he differed from me in any important particular. At the close of our interview he said he would prepare his report to the Secretary, and show it to me before forwarding it. My recollection of this is clear and distinct, and I know I cannot be mistaken in regard to it.

Thus matters remained till I received an unofficial letter from Mr. Chase, of which the following is a copy : —

" TREASURY DEPARTMENT, February 12th, 1864.

" My dear Sir : — I inclose an official letter which speaks for itself. General Dix feels greatly hurt by the removal of his brother, and wishes that I would examine the matter anew. I cannot do this, and do justice to you at the same time, without conferring with you personally. I therefore desire to see you in Washington. I hope it will not be inconvenient for you to come. There are many subjects I shall be glad to confer with you about.

"Very truly yours,   S. P. CHASE.

" J. Z. GOODRICH, Esq., Boston, Mass."

I went to Washington, as requested, where I found, among the papers in the case, Mr. Hooper's report. This was the first intimation I had that it had been made. It was dated September 15th, 1863, a short time after his interview with me at the Custom House. It closed with the statement that *" the Collector declined to confer with me (him) on the subject,"* which I pronounce to be utterly and inexcusably false. Mr. Hooper knew better. Inclosed with his report I found a letter to him, written, as the report states, at his request, from R. S. S. Andros, Esq., dated September 7th, also the affidavit of Mr. Payne, dated August 22d, and of Mr. T. B. Dix, dated September 7th, 1863. I also found a letter from General Dix to the Secretary, dated November 20, 1863, in which he spoke of the ordering of an " investigation," and thus referred to Mr. Hooper's report : —
" The Hon. Mr. Hooper has made his report, and I am told my brother is completely vindicated. I now ask, as an act of justice, that he may be placed in the position which he occupied before his unjust removal by Mr. Goodrich. * * Mr. Harrington (Assistant Secretary) assured me that he should not be considered out of place, and that the result of the investigation should be *decisive."* Perhaps Mr. Hooper had received the same assurance from Mr. Harrington, which may explain why he *forgot* to show me his report: Its conclusions do " completely vindicate " Mr. Dix, and it was doubtless expected Mr. Chase would treat it as decisive without explanation from me. But he thought justice to me required a personal conference, and he sought one.

Mr. Chase said he must see Mr. Hooper and myself together, and proposed to meet us at 10 o'clock the next morning at his office. We met at the time appointed. Perhaps two hours were spent in verbal statements by Mr. Hooper in explanation and vindication of his report, and in replies by me pointing out what seemed to be not errors merely, but perversions both of fact and law, to which Mr. Chase listened.

MR. HOOPER'S REPORT.

, It conclusively shows that he knew the cargo was all warehoused on or before the 26th of July. It says : — " The entry and order to receive into warehouse, was for rum, sugar, and molasses ; the rum was put into the store on the 25th July ; the next day, being Saturday, the 26th July, Messrs. Chenery & Co. sold the sugar and molasses at auction, and immediately entered it out, paid the duty, and received the delivery permit ; which permit they took to the Storekeeper on the morning of the next business day, which was Monday, the 28th July."

If the next business day *after* they received the permit was Monday the 28th, of course they received it Saturday the 26th.   Mr.

Hooper admits, then, that Chenery & Co. paid the duties on the sugar and molasses, and " entered it out " of warehouse, or withdrew it *from* warehouse, on Saturday the 26th, and the same day received a permit or order for it, as was the fact. Consequently he *knew* it had been *previously* warehoused, as otherwise it could not have been withdrawn *from* warehouse. And he states, substantially, the same thing in another passage, as follows : —

" The sugar and molasses, after having been entered for storage, could be obtained for delivery to the purchasers, only by entering it out, as if it was actually in the warehouse; for this purpose only *is it considered constructively in the warehouse while on the wharf.*"

This admits it was constructively in the warehouse while on the wharf. And if it could be obtained for delivery only by entering it out, and could be entered out only when constructively (if not actually) in the warehouse, and if it *was* in the warehouse for this purpose, as Mr. Hooper says it was, then it must have been warehoused, *as he must have known*, BEFORE it was " entered out " on the 26th. Nothing further can be needed on this point.

And the evidence of the facts presented to Chenery & Co., Dix and Payne at the time the rum was withdrawn on the 28th of October, or of what they *then* knew, agrees perfetly with this admission of Mr. Hooper. This his report sufficiently shows. It says : —

" As it appears by the Storekeeper's return " (agreeing exactly with the Inspector's return), " that the deposit in the warehouse was made on the 25th July, consequently that it had been in the Warehouse more than three months, the warehouse Book-keeper, Mr. H. A. S. D. Payne, decided that the rum" (there was but one return, showing the rum, sugar, and molasses were deposited at the same time), " was subject to duty at the rate of one hundred and eighteen cents per gallon under the law of July 14th, 1862." (They knew, it seems, what the law was). * * " On referring " (Chenery & Co. referred) " to the principal Storage Clerk, Mr. T. B. Dix, he stated that the return of the Storekeeper must be their guide, and that the rum could not be withdrawn without paying the duty at the rate of one hundred and eighteen cents per gallon."

It is manifest, therefore, they all knew the goods were warehoused according to the returns, on the 25th of July, and they knew the withdrawal of the sugar and molasses by Chenery & Co. the next day — which the withdrawal entry in the Custom House showed — proved the correctness of the returns, as the withdrawal could not have been made if the warehousing had not been previously made. With this proof that the returns were correct, — proof by their own withdrawal entry, — Chenery & Co. went right to work to get the date of warehousing altered.

And this brings me to another part of Mr. Hooper's report, made for another purpose (which will appear as we proceed), in which he pretends, and upon a theory quite new, attempts to show that the sugar and molasses were *not warehoused*, actually or constructively, till the 28th of July. Portions of this part of his report, taken in connection with the quotations already made, are curiosities. He says : —

" Messrs. Chenery & Co. claimed that the return was erroneous, as the date of deposit in the warehouse was the 28th instead of the 25th of July, * * * * Messrs. Chenery & Co. went to the public warehouse, and, after some conversation with the Storekeeper who made the return, in regard to the facts

In the case, requested him to go to the Custom House and consult the principal Clerk, Mr. T. B. Dix, and the warehouse Book-keeper, Mr. H. A. S. D. Payne, both of whom had more experience than the Storekeeper in regard to what had been the usual practice in relation to the return of goods deposited in the public warehouse. After hearing the statement of the Storekeeper" (which was that the goods were all warehoused on the 25th July, — it has never been pretended that he ever made a different statement), "Mr. Dix expressed the opinion that upon *his statement of the facts, in accordance with the usual practice, the return should have been dated the 28th of July instead of the 26th; also, that it would be right for the Storekeeper to alter his return so as to make it conform to the facts in the case.* The Storekeeper then changed the return by altering the date from the 26th to the 28th July, and in the body of the return so that instead of stating the deposit in warehouse to be on the 25th July, it was stated to have been received on the 25th and 28th July; thereby naming the first and last days, as had been customary in such returns, viz., the date of the receipt of the first package in warehouse as the first, and for the other the last day on which any of the goods were received in the warehouse. Messrs. Chenery & Co. entered the rum on the 28th of October after this *correction* of the return had been made, and paid the duty at the rate of fifty-nine cents a gallon."

More uncandid or groundless assumptions than these were never made. The Storekeeper's return was not altered to *correct* it; nobody concerned in the transaction could have supposed it was. And Mr. Hooper must have known it conformed exactly to the facts in the case. At any rate, he *knew* that the sugar and molasses were *withdrawn* on the 26th, and that they had been warehoused *before* they were withdrawn. And he knew the rum was warehoused on the 25th, for he so states. Nor was the cargo warehoused on *different* days, as assumed. Mr. Hooper knew it was all warehoused, if ever, on the *same* day. This not only the Storekeeper's return, but the Inspector's return showed, both of which were in his hands, or copies. The report proceeds : —

" To arrive at a correct conclusion from the statement of the facts presented in this case, the first question to be considered is whether the 28th of July was the true date that should have been originally returned; and secondly, if it was the true date, whether it was proper to make the alteration in the return. In answering these questions it seems to me that the usual practice of the Boston Custom House should be considered, and not what was abstractly the most correct and judicious action in regard to such returns."

But how does he attempt to prove that the 28th was the true date that should have been returned as the date of deposit in warehouse? In this way, in his own words : —

"When, after having been entered for warehousing, any portion of the goods specified in the entry is entered out before it has been sent to the warehouse, as was the case in this transaction of Chenery & Co., *the time when the delivery permit is received by the Storekeeper, is considered the final date of deposit*" (in warehouse).

This means that when the duties are paid on part of a lot of goods entered for warehousing, and it is withdrawn while it remains in the possession of the Storekeeper on the wharf before being actually sent to the warehouse, and the owners have received an order for it, the time when this order or delivery permit is presented to the Storekeeper is to be considered the time of final deposit in warehouse, whether one, two, ten, thirty days or months after the withdrawal entry or payment of the duties (in this case two days after). In other words, the time of actual delivery *out*, or the time the Storekeeper "receives" from the owners the order to deliver out, is the time of final deposit *in* warehouse. Can anything be more absurd? There is no connection whatever between the two transactions. The order to *receive* is before the duties are paid. The order to *deliver* is after the duties are paid. They are signed by different officers and issued from different departments. Moreover, the order to receive into warehouse *must* first be executed before the order to deliver *can* be regularly issued. How, then, can anybody but feel surprised that a man of Mr. Hooper's intelligence, who has been so many years engaged in the importing business, and so long familiar with the mode of passing goods through the Custom House, should make such a statement as this. That it is wholly unfounded, cannot admit of a doubt.

Besides, the time when goods are legally withdrawn is, not when the owners receive them from the warehouse, or present an order for them, but when *the duties are paid* on the withdrawal entry. Secretary Chase, doubtless, surprised at Mr. Hooper's pretence of any such custom as he talked about, inquired of the Collector of New York when goods are withdrawn from warehouse, who replied under date of February 2d, 1864, as follows : —

"I regard the *payment of the duties* on the withdrawal entry, as the *actual act* of withdrawal from warehouse, *no matter when thereafter the order was presented to the Storekeeper.*"

From the nature of the case it must be so. What has the Government to do with imported merchandise after the duties are paid? Nothing, of course. Manifestly they should not be warehoused, actually or constructively, after that, and as a matter of fact and practice, well known to all importers, they are not. And yet Mr. Hooper tells the Secretary that according to the custom or "usual practice" of the Boston Custom House, they are.

The position of Mr. Hooper that an importer may keep his order for withdrawn and duty paid goods in his pocket till it suits his convenience to present it, with the understanding that the time of presenting it will fix the date of warehousing goods not withdrawn and duties not paid, and extend the time within which they may be withdrawn without additional duty (as in this case on the rum from the 25th to the 28th), is simply preposterous, and it would be an impeachment of his intelligence to suppose for a moment that he does not know it is.

But he tries still further to justify this position by saying that the Storekeeper "could not properly return on the 26th July that he had received the rum, sugar and molasses into the warehouse." Not proper to make the return on the 26th! How is it possible Mr. Hooper can justify such a statement? It was not only proper the return should be made when it was, but it was *necessary* to enable Chenery & Co. to withdraw the sugar and molasses on the 26th. If there had been no return, there would have been no evidence at the Custom House that the sugar and molasses had been warehoused. But the return had been made. The Storekeeper's return stated that the goods had been "received into store on the 25th." The Inspector's return stated that they had been "warehoused or stored on the 25th."

This was the *required* evidence to the Collector thàt the goods were "in the warehouse" and might be withdrawn. The Storekeeper's return, therefore, was properly made *before* they were withdrawn and the delivery permit issued. Can it be that Mr. Hooper, an old importer, could be ignorant of this? And it was undoubtedly made early in the day *for the very purpose of enabling Chenery & Co.*, after the auction sale, to make the withdrawal entry and get the delivery , permit, and it being properly made, it was of course properly dated the 26th, *when* made. Nothing can show more clearly than this , simple statement of the regular and necessary order of proceeding, the iniquity of the pretence that the goods were not warehoused till the 28th.

And Mr. Hooper even goes so far, in this part of his report, as to say that " the Storekeeper had no control over the sugar and molasses on the wharf." His own words, already quoted, are a sufficient answer to this. He says, "the sugar and molasses, after having been entered for storage, *could* be obtained for delivery to the purchasers *only* by entering it out." Why not, if the Storekeeper had no control over it? Why might not Chenery & Co., if this was so, have taken it without paying duty and without a permit? Could this be done? Of course it could not. The Storekeeper might at any moment, as Mr. Hooper ought to have known, have sent the sugar and molasses to the store. Suppose Chenery & Co. had changed their minds, and decided not to sell, pay the duties, and withdraw from warehouse for two months, can it be pretended that the Storekeeper could not have controlled it and put it into store? He not only might have done this, but it would have been his duty to do it.

TIMOTHY B. DIX.

Mr. Hooper represents Mr. Dix as saying that "upon the Storekeeper's statement of the facts, in accordance with the usual practice, the return should have been dated the 28th of July instead of the 26th, and that it would be proper to alter it."

He said this and more. He directed the alteration. But it was wholly immaterial, so far as Mr. Dix was concerned, what the Storekeeper stated. He knew the facts as well as anybody could tell him. He had been in the Custom House, and in that very office, seventeen years, and was perfectly familiar with every paper. He knew the deposit and Storekeeper's return were properly and regularly made before Chenery & Co. withdrew the sugar and molasses, and therefore that the return could not properly be *dated* two days after the withdrawal. He must have known there was no such usual practice as he spoke of, and never had been. He knew, or ought to have known, that the Storekeeper's return, if altered, would contradict the Inspector's return, and would be *incorrect* as soon as altered, and yet he directed the alteration to be made on purpose to aid in carrying out the plan devised to give Chenery & Co. their rum by paying half the lawful duty. Mr. Dix knew the importation was made the 24th of July, because he himself issued the order that very day, after entry and importation, to the Storekeeper to receive the cargo, which order was before him when the alteration in the return was made. In a word, there was not a material fact that he did not know perfectly. In his affidavit there is not a word which relates to the question.

4

R. S. S. ANDROS'S LETTER.

In his letter to Mr. Hooper, it appears that Mr. Andros understood the facts. He then says : — "I entertain no doubt that, under the practice, the 28th was the proper date of deposit." And I entertain no doubt that he ought to be heartily ashamed of having expressed such an opinion. A man who had been as familiar with Custom House matters as he had, ought to have known better.

CHENERY & CO.'S LETTER.

The official letter inclosed in the Secretary's unofficial note of the 12th of February, was Chenery & Co.'s, dated December 31, 1863. It was a request to the Secretary to order a refund of the additional duty, for reasons stated. The following are extracts from it : —

" We respectfully represent that on the 24th of July, 1862, we imported into this District a cargo of merchandise * * and entered the whole cargo for warehousing in one entry. Said cargo, according to the officer's return, *and in accordance with the facts in the case,* was deposited in warehouse *from the 25th to the 28th of July,* 1862. The whole of the merchandise was *immediately* withdrawn *from* warehouse, excepting an invoice of forty-eight puncheons of rum."

These are extraordinary statements, and wholly at variance with the known facts in the case. That the rum was deposited in warehouse on the 25th there is no dispute. When, therefore, they assert that according to the facts in the case the cargo was deposited in warehouse from the 25th *to the* 28th, they mean to say that *according to the facts* the sugar and molasses were deposited on the 28th. And yet they themselves withdrew the "whole" of it from warehouse on the 26th of July, having paid the duties on it, which, of course, they knew. They certainly had the means of knowing it. They could have ascertained from their own books that they paid the duty on the 26th ; and the date of their withdrawal entry, which was in the Custom House, would have shown at any time that that also was made on the 26th. And on the same day they received the order for the goods, and they knew they presented it to the Storekeeper on the 28th and took them *out* of warehouse, and did *not* put them *into* warehouse. The question of time being the very question to settle, it is not a supposable case that when they proposed to withdraw the rum on the 28th of October, they could have *forgotten* to ascertain when they paid the duty, made their withdrawal entry, and received the delivery permit.

Chenery & Co. are especially inexcusable in persisting in representations so palpably false, eight months after the discovery of the fraud, and there is no way of accounting for it except upon the expectation that the Secretary would adopt the conclusions and recommendations of Mr. Hooper's report without much inquiry or examination. They doubtless had been informed of the report, and of Assistant Secretary Harrington's assurance to General Dix, that the result of the investigation should be "decisive."

. The 28th of July, the time they pretend the deposit was made, was two days after the duties on the sugar and molasses had been paid, and nobody knows better than Chenery & Co. that the Government does not receive goods into warehouse, actually or constructively, after the duties are paid.

MR. HOOPER'S LAW.

But the law of July 14th, 1862, was yet to be got over with the Secretary. This was done by Mr. Hooper in two ways. First, he says, —

"In regard to the law of July 14th, 1862, subjecting goods in public warehouses to an increase of duty when entered for consumption, after three months from the date of *importation*, it is not clearly established by law in this country, as it is in England, what time constitutes the *date* of importation."

He means, if he means anything by this, to say that it was not clearly established by law in this country that these goods, on the 28th of October, (for he is applying it to the present case), had been imported three months. He admits it was three months and *four* days after Chenery & Co. entered them at the Custom House, viz., on the 24th of July, and swore that the importation was then made, and three months and *three* days after the goods had *all* been landed and the rum actually put into Government store, viz., on the 25th of July, and yet he doubts whether it is clearly established by law in *this country* — he thinks it is in England — that all this constitutes an *importation*, or the *date* of importation, before the 28th of July. This is the opinion of *the* member of Congress who claims to have suggested and framed this very change in the law.

But second, fearing after all that this might constitute an importation, he proceeded to lay before the Secretary his *understanding* — entirely erroneous — of the construction of the law at the Custom House, and the practice under it. He says : —

"I understand that no change was made in the practice at the Custom House in Boston in consequence of this change in the phraseology of the law; that the *date of importation* was construed to mean the same as *the date of deposit* in previous laws."

What Mr. Hooper *understood*, of course I cannot say, but nothing could be more erroneous than what he states. The change was made the very day the law went into operation. Mr. Deputy Hanscom's attention was specially called to the alteration ; in fact he was consulted in Washington in regard to it just before it was made, and he changed the practice at once. This Mr. Hooper might easily have ascertained, and it was his duty to have ascertained it before making such a report to the Secretary. He certainly had no business to make a statement in regard to it contrary to the fact.*

---

* CUSTOM HOUSE, NEW YORK, }
Collector's Office, May 14, 1866. }

Sir : — In reply to your letter of the 12th inst. I have to state that I was in Washington in the latter part of June and first of July, 1862, that while at the Treasury Department, Mr. George Wood showed me a proposed tariff bill printed by Congress, and requested me to suggest any alterations which occurred to me. Among other things, I advised that the words 'date of original importation' where it appears in the 21st section, should be inserted in lieu of the words 'date of deposit in warehouse or public store,' or words to that effect (the exact words I do not now remember), similar to the provision in the 5th section of the act of August 5, 1861.

My suggestions, with the reasons therefor, were reduced to writing at the request of Mr. Wood, a clerk in the Treasury Department.

As soon as the act reached me after its passage, I examined it to ascertain if the suggestion had been acted upon, because it had proved inconven-

" In regard to alterations of returns " (I quote from Mr. Hooper's report) " by officers after they have been handed into the Custom House, I am told that it is constantly occurring in regard to dates, marks, or other details where facts are incorrectly stated." There is not a circumstance to justify the assumption that the facts were *incorrectly* stated, and it is embarrassing to know how to characterize it. But even if they had been incorrectly stated, Chenery & Co. should have sought a remedy in another way. But the truth is, a correct return was *pretended* to be incorrect, and thus a foundation was laid to correct a pretended inaccuracy, and the correction was made for a fraudulent purpose. If this is not to be classed among the gravest of Custom House offences, then I do not know where to class it. Mr. Dix's first excuse, when I called him to an account, was, that nothing was more common than these alterations,—they were made every day. This surprised me, and I asked him to explain what he meant. His explanation was simply and only this: that officers—Storekeepers and Inspectors—who make these returns, on discovering in a day or two, on entry, that they have made a mistake in the count and find one or more packages short, or over, as the case may be, are allowed to correct it. Said I, " Mr. Dix, do you justify the alteration of dates that are more than three months' old, and that, too, for the purpose of falsifying a correct date and relieving an importer from half the duty, because corrections such as you have now described are allowed?" He admitted there was a wide difference in the cases.

Mr. Hooper says: " Messrs. Chenery & Co. are gentlemen of high character." I do not controvert this, but men of high character, even, have no right to defraud the Government in the way they attempted to. He also speaks of the " high character of Mr. Dix as a faithful officer." In this transaction no man could have been more unfaithful.

At length, after we had gone over the points and I had read the law to Mr. Chase, he said: " One thing is clear, the law is as Mr. Goodrich states it, and the money paid for the additional duty cannot be refunded to Chenery & Co. As to Mr. Dix, he can be excused, if at all, only on the ground of a custom or ' usual practice ' which Mr. Hooper says existed." I quote his words as near as I can.

Something then occurred to prevent Mr. Chase from considering the matter further at that time, and he requested us to meet him at the same place at ten the next morning. I met the Secretary at the time appointed, but Mr. Hooper did not appear. After a few minutes conversation upon the alleged custom or " usual practice," in which I stated that no such custom existed, or had ever existed, so far as I knew ; that I never heard of it till I saw Mr. Hooper's report, and that his statements in regard to it were wholly unfounded and erroneous, Mr. Chase interrupted me by saying: " I am satisfied, Mr.

---

ient to keep a correct account of the date of deposit of goods in bonded warehouse, while the date of original importation was a fixed and certain record made on arrival of the vessel. Finding the alteration had been made, as Deputy Collector, having in charge the warehouse business at the Custom House, I gave the necessary directions required by the change.

I am, very truly, your friend and ob't servant,
ALBERT HANSCOM.
Hon. J. Z. Goodrich, Boston.

Goodrich, *that there was no such custom,* and if there had been *and you had known it, it would have been good cause for removing you.*" These, I think, are his very words. I responded simply by saying "Certainly it would," and Mr. Chase immediately dictated, in my hearing, a letter to General Dix announcing the result of his further investigation of his brother's case, which was that "Mr. Goodrich was right in removing him, and he could not interfere in his behalf." This was the substance of his letter, which I supposed would be an end of the matter. But it was not.

GENERAL DIX COMPLAINED TO MR. FESSENDEN.

Not long after Mr. Fessenden succeeded Mr. Chase as Secretary of the Treasury, General Dix complained to him that his brother had been unjustly removed from office in the Boston Custom House, and demanded that he should be reinstated. Mr. Fessenden, after requesting the General to call the next day, sent for the clerk who had charge of the papers and was acquainted with the history of the case, and asked him if Mr. Chase's decision was made after a careful inquiry into the facts ; and upon being assured that it was, he directed him to take the papers back. The General called the next day, and was told by Mr. Fessenden that he could not reopen a case of removal by a Collector which had the approval of his predecessor in the first instance, and his added subsequent approval after a full and careful examination upon a re-hearing. Of this I knew nothing at the time, but I have the highest authority for saying the facts are substantially as stated.

GENERAL DIX APPEALED TO MR. McCULLOCH.

At length Mr. Fessenden resigned, and Mr. McCulloch was appointed Secretary, from whom I received a letter of which the following is a copy : —

"TREASURY DEPARTMENT, June 9, 1865.

"Dear Sir : — I have received a communication from General Dix, of New York, in relation to the removal of his brother, Mr. T. B. Dix, from the Custom House in Boston in the year 1861 (1863).

"From an examination of the papers submitted by General Dix, and *a report by Mr. Hooper,* member of Congress from your city, upon the charges presented, I am *clearly of the opinion* that injustice was done to a worthy man in this removal, and I have therefore to ask that Mr. Dix be *reinstated in the place from which he was removed.*

"I am very respectfully,

"H. McCULLOCH, Secretary of Treasury.

"J. Z. GOODRICH, Esq., Collector, Boston, Mass."

"An examination of the papers submitted by General Dix, and a report of Mr. Hooper," but no examination of the reports I had made, so far as appears, nor a word of explanation asked from me. It seemed to me a little remarkable, to say the least, that I should receive so summary a request under all the circumstances of this case, to reinstate Mr. Dix. The following is an extract from my reply, dated June 12th : —

"Dear Sir : — I have your favor of the 9th instant. I think I can place myself right in this matter, without going fully into its merits, which would require a long letter. The removal was approved by your predecessor, Mr. Secretary, now Chief Justice, Chase. Afterwards General Dix claimed that injustice had been done his brother, and made, probably, the same statements to Mr. Chase that he has made to you, and requested that the case might be inquired into by the Secretary again, who addressed me a private note desiring that I would go to Washington and make a full explanation to him. I accordingly went to Washington, where I saw for the first time the papers furnished by General Dix, and Mr. Hooper's report, * * * Mr. Chase said he must see Mr. Hooper and myself together, * * We met at the time appointed. Mr. Hooper made a full verbal explanation, in addition to his report. I replied, and pointed out the facts, &c. * * Mr. Chase remarked that Mr. Dix could only be excused, if at all, on the ground of the custom which Mr. Hooper claimed existed at the Custom House. I remarked that no such custom existed, or ought to exist. Here the interview for that day closed, with the understanding that we would meet the Secretary again next morning. I accordingly called the next morning, but, if I remember right, Mr. Hooper did not. I explained in regard to the alleged custom, and denied that there was any custom of the kind. Mr. Chase remarked, ' I am satisfied there was no such custom, and if there had been and you had known it, it would have been a good reason for removing you for allowing it.' This ended the interview, and the Secretary at once, in my hearing, dictated a letter to General Dix justifying my course in the removal of his brother, and declining to interfere.

" I state this as the result to which the then Secretary came after an unusually thorough examination of the case. * * He approved of the appointment of another man in his place, who has performed its duties ever since. What am I to do with him, appointed with the approval of Mr. Chase, if I am to reinstate Mr. Dix?

" P. S. I am sure Mr. Chase will confirm the foregoing, in substance."

My only purpose in this letter was to show that the case had been carefully and thoroughly considered by Mr. Chase. Mr. McCulloch's reply was as follows : —

" TREASURY DPARTMENT, June 16, 1865.
"Dear Sir : — Your favor of the 12th instant is received. General Dix in his communications with this office, charges that his brother was removed, not for improper conduct on his part, but because he failed to obtain for a relative of yours a position in the Custom House at New York.

" The charge is made without reservation, and a letter from you to General Dix, under date July 11, 1861, is referred to in connection with a letter of Mr. Barney, dated September 7th, '61, as establishing the charge.

" General Dix urges very strongly, and very plausibly, that the only way in which justice can be done to his brother is by having him reinstated in the office from which he was removed.

" Unless you are prepared to disprove the charge referred to, it would be no more than simple justice to Mr. Dix that he be reinstated in his former office, although in reinstating him you will be under the necessity of displacing an officer who was appointed with the approval of Mr. Chase.
" I am very respectfully,
"H. McCULLOCH, Secretary of the Treasury.
" J. Z. GOODRICH, Esq., Collector of Customs, Boston, Mass."

My reply to this very extraordinary letter, was as follows : —

" COLLECTOR'S OFFICE,
" Custom House, Boston, 19th June, 1865.
" Dear Sir : — Your favor of the 16th is just received. By it I am informed for the first time, that General Dix charges that his brother was removed, not from improper conduct on his part, but because he failed to obtain for a relative of yours (mine) a position in the Custom House at New York. In this the General is utterly mistaken. * * I never had the slightest feeling against General Dix on the subject, nor against his brother. I always supposed he did all he properly could to obtain the appointment of my friend. My recollection is that the suggestion was well received by the General; that he applied to Mr. Barney in my friend's behalf, and I always understood the reason why the appointment was not made was, that Mr. Barney did not see his way clear to appoint a Massachusetts man. He wrote me on the subject, and

assigned that as his reason. Such is now my recollection, though the letters are none of them before me; indeed, I do not think I preserved them, never expecting to have occasion to refer to them again.

"Furthermore, the friend alluded to had received an appointment from me nearly a year before Mr. Dix was removed.

"Not long after I was appointed Collector, Mr. Chase, in a private note, at the request, as he said, of General Dix, asked me not to remove his brother. He was as subject to removal on political grounds, having been a Buchanan Democrat, as any one, and his removal was expected undoubtedly — certainly feared — on this ground. When I received Mr. C.'s note I abandoned all thought of removing him, till the facts which I assigned as a reason for doing it finally came to my knowledge. Nor did I do it then without presenting the facts to Mr. Chase and obtaining his opinion, which was done in this way. Mr. Tuck, the Naval Officer, happened to be going to Washington just about that time, and I gave him the original papers which contained the evidence of the impropriety complained of, and asked him to explain the matter to Mr. Chase. Mr. Tuck informed me that Mr. Chase's opinion was that the officers concerned in the transaction should be removed, and that he desired me to send a copy of the papers to the Department. I then made the removal, and forwarded copies of the papers as requested, with my reasons. The removal was at once approved. · The case was further investigated by Mr. Chase after this.

"I am prepared to disprove the charge referred to, and also to convince you that the cause of removal, — *if you desire to open the question after it was so thoroughly considered by the then Secretary,* — was sufficient, and will go to Washington for that purpose if you desire it."

No reply to this letter was received, nor was I invited to Washington to make explanations. At length, however, I went to Washington, and on the 10th of August saw the Secretary for the first time at his office. After a few words of introduction, I at once introduced the Dix case. He said he did not wish to hear anything further on the subject. I replied that he had come to the clear opinion from reading Mr. Hooper's report that I had done injustice to Mr. Dix, and I thought he should at least hear what I had to say. He replied that he did not wish to go into the matter; that it was unnecessary, &c. I insisted that after saying what he had in his letter, it was due to me that he listened to my explanations, and told him I had prepared a written statement, which, if he preferred, he could take and read at his convenience, which would not occupy more than fifteen or twenty minutes. He said no, he did not care to read it. I again urged that he owed it to me personally to do as much as this. He said he was disposed to do any thing he could for me personally, but no good could come from a further discussion of that case, and declined even to read what I had prepared. I said if you positively decline, I shall of course be obliged to submit. After some further conversation on the subject, he at length said: "It is unnecessary to go into the question, for I have conferred with Mr. Bailey, who has satisfied me *that you are right about it.*"

And who is Mr. Bailey?. He is Mr. J. F. Bailey who was special agent of the Department under Mr. Chase and Mr. Fessenden, and under Mr. McCulloch also till a short time before, when he was appointed Collector of Internal Revenue in the city of New York, which office he holds now.

Some time after Mr. Hooper's report, but before I had seen it or knew it was made, — not far from the first of December, 1863, — Mr. Bailey, who had spent several weeks in examining other matters in the Boston Custom House, was requested by Mr. Chase, to examine and report upon the Dix case also. He commenced the examination with a strong personal desire that the matter might be arranged satisfactorily to General Dix, and hoped to find a state of facts that would justify a report exonerating his brother. I laid before him all the facts, and explained them just as I had done to Mr. Hooper.* At the close of his investigation he told me he was sorry to be obliged to say that I could not restore Mr. Dix consistently with my duty as a public officer, nor with my self-respect, and that he should so state to Mr. Chase. I suppose he made a report to that effect, but I never saw it.

After all this it would seem to be quite time Mr. McCulloch came to the conclusion that I was right about it, or *possibly might be.* And yet, satisfied of this, as he admitted finally, soon after Mr. Hamlin was appointed Collector, he requested him to put Mr. Dix back into the office from which he was removed. This, I understand, Mr. Hamlin declined to do, but said, in substance, that he would appoint him to another office if the Secretary, after the decisions which had been made by his predecessors, desired it. In this way he threw the responsibility upon the Secretary, and at his request appointed Mr. Dix an additional Aid to the Revenue. In other words, an office was *created* for Mr. Dix, and it ought to be known that he received it at the request and on the responsibility of the Secretary, and that, too, after he became *satisfied that I was right about this case,* and of course that his predecessor, Mr. Chase, was right.

A word should be added in explanation of the request to General Dix to favor an appointment in the New York Custom House from Massachusetts. I wrote him that in accordance with Mr. Chase's request I should retain his brother, but added that I was urged to remove him on the ground, in part, that he came from New York, and was occupying a place which fairly belonged to some one in Massachusetts. As an answer to this I asked him to request Collector Barney to appoint some one from Massachusetts whom I should recommend. After Mr. Barney wrote me, I thought no more of it. These, with those before stated, are the substantial facts as I remember them, and if General Dix has any letters from me which prove, or tend to prove his charge, he is at perfect liberty to publish them. I am willing the world should know all I have said or written about this matter. But General Dix has no letter of mine which will prove his charge. It is obvious his purpose was to withdraw attention from his brother by getting up a personal issue with me. His charge is utterly false. He has not a particle of excuse for making it. And the attempt to divert attention from the charge against his brother, which Mr. Chase, against every personal wish and desire, had been forced to sustain, by pretending to *another* Secretary that I was influenced.by unworthy personal motives growing out of an affair of no consequence which I

* Extract of a letter from Mr. Bailey to me, dated May 16, 1866 : —

" The details of the case of Mr. Timothy B. Dix, and of the inquiries made in it by me, under direction of the then Secretary, have in great part passed from my mind, but in reply to your request that I state whether you exhibited all the papers, and showed a disposition to render every facility for a full examination, *I am clear that all my impressions as to your own course were to that effect.*"

had forgotten, is especially mean and cowardly. And the time spent by Mr. McCulloch in *this mode* of reviewing the decisions of his predecessors, it is quite safe to say will be very poorly spent. If he had told General Dix to prove his charge, made without " reservation," before calling on me to " disprove " it, the proceeding would have been much more regular.

Many will wonder how Mr. Hooper could have expected that Mr. Chase would ever approve such a report as his. The truth undoubtedly is, he had no expectation Mr. Chase would ever examine his report. If he had, he certainly would have made a different one. His expectation unquestionably was that the matter would be settled by Mr. Harrington, the Assistant Secretary. With him there would have been no difficulty. His assurance had been obtained that the result of the investigation should be " decisive."

The fact that Mr. Chase requested Mr. Hooper to report upon the case, implied that he had confidence that he would make a fair and true report. He said nothing to me except this : " *I am satisfied, Mr. Goodrich, there was no such custom* (as Mr. Hooper claimed existed), *and if there had been, and you had known it, it would have been good cause for removing you.*" This he said, and of course did not rely on Mr. Hooper's statements, doubtless feeling that the confidence he had placed in him had been misplaced.

MR. HOOPER AND SECRETARY McCULLOCH ON BAGGAGE-SMUGGLING BY THE RESPECTABLE AND. WEALTHY.

The law exempts from duty " wearing apparel in actual use," only, " and other personal effects, not merchandise."

The construction given this law by the Department heretofore has been, that articles that might be admitted free as " wearing apparel," were " limited to such as it shall be satisfactorily shown *had been* in actual use of the person bringing it into the United States." (Treasury Circular, April 12th, 1847.)

And the meaning of " personal effects " is thus stated : —

" The general description of personal effects, that they are such as are usually carried about the person of a traveller from place to place, is a very good one, and is adopted by this Department. It includes his trunk, his watch, his pen-knife, his pencil or pen, his stationery, his razors, &c.; in short, every thing appertaining to his person, not merchandise." (Circular Instructions, September 28th, 1843.)

A circular was issued by the Department August 6th, 1864, specially enjoining it upon Collectors to be vigilant in the execution of this law. The following is an extract from it : —

" The examination of travellers' baggage will, under any circumstances, be a very unpleasant and annoying duty; nevertheless, *it must be performed.*"

The following are extracts from another circular of instructions to Collectors from the Department, July 25th, 1865 : —

" Customs officers seem to entertain great fears, lest they should hurt some one's feelings, or be thought to do their duty too rigidly, and the result is, that they are laughed at behind their backs by immigrants and passengers, who very often succeed in getting various dutiable articles through without paying duty, of more or less, sometimes of considerable value. I shall be glad to know that you have no such squeamish officers among your subordinates. The Government can dispense with the services of all such. He who has not resolution and high sense of duty enough to overhaul the baggage, even of ladies, who are often smugglers, is unfit for his place."

Such were the views of the Department, and such its recent instructions in regard to the execution of this law.

On the 19th of August, 1864, a gentleman and three ladies arrived in the steamer from Europe. The gentleman made a written declaration that their trunks contained " clothing for three ladies and one gentleman," which he handed to the officer whose duty it was to receive it. This was done, as was apparent from what followed, with the expectation that the declaration would be accepted and the trunks allowed to pass without examination. The officer inquired whether they contained any *dutiable* articles, or anything besides *clothing in use*, and was told that they *did not*. The trunks were then passed on to another officer for examination. He soon found articles that were dutiable. The gentleman then said, " Do you examine so particularly as that?" When informed that the instructions were to examine sufficiently to ascertain whether there were any dutiable articles, he then said there was a " considerable quantity of new goods," and requested that the trunks might be sent to the Appraisers and opened there, as he wanted them handled carefully. This request was at once complied with. All this occurred before I heard of the case, and I never saw either the trunks, or the clothing, or the new goods.

The next morning, before I knew whether the examination had been made at the Appraisers, Mr. Hooper called on me at the Collector's office in a perfect rage of passion. He was very angry. I have rarely seen a man more angry. Coming up to my desk he demanded the trunks of the ladies and gentlemen, naming them. I replied that I knew very little about the circumstances of their detention, and must have more information before I could act in the matter. He walked back and forth, growing more excited, if possible, and said they had been sent to the Appraisers, and repeated his demand. I said again I could give no order till I had more information. This did not satisfy him, and he again demanded the immediate delivery of the trunks. I replied — somewhat in earnest by this time myself, — that they had been sent to the Appraisers by the Inspector for further examination, and properly, as it was my duty to suppose, and that he might rest assured, I should give no order for them till I received the report of the Appraiser, at the same time assuring him of no disposition to detain them a moment unnecessarily. Soon, while we were yet talking, the Appraiser's report was sent in to me. Without waiting to read the items I saw that it was made by R. K. Darrah, Assistant Appraiser, who certified to $568.85 of dutiable goods at the foreign value, and to $219.79 duties upon them, and told Mr. Hooper that I could not decide upon the case till I had learned all the facts, but was willing to order a delivery of the trunks with all their contents, if he would sign on the back of the appraisement the following, to which he finally agreed : —

"I agree to pay such sums to J. Z. Goodrich, Collector, as may be found to be due from (inserting the name) either as forfeiture, penalty, or duty, for bringing the goods into this port in his baggage which are described within.
(Signed)   S. HOOPER.
"Boston, August 20th, 1864."

During our interview Mr. Hooper had a great deal to say about the impropriety of presuming to examine the baggage of respectable people who were above suspicion. His repeated demands were based on that impropriety. The law did not mean that people of respectability and character should be annoyed in this way. My reply, in substance, was that the law and my instructions were, neither to annoy or detain anybody unnecessarily, but to examine the baggage of everybody so far as necessary to ascertain whether it contained dutiable goods ; that if respectable people brought dutiable articles in their baggage, there seemed to be no reason why they, especially, should be allowed to pass them without paying the duty.

Mr. Hooper at length complained to the Secretary in behalf of his friends, and of the manner this law was being executed at the Boston Custom House. This I learned from Mr. French, the late Deputy, who was so informed at the Department. Finally, on the 19th of August, 1865, I wrote the Secretary, and after reciting the principal facts, added : —

"The owners of the baggage, very respectable citizens of Boston, complained that the trunks were not allowed to pass without examination, and others, friends of theirs, who are influential citizens, have censured me severely for the course that was taken. The case is not disposed of, and I take the liberty of presenting it to you, as my orders came from you. I suppose the course pursued by my officers was the course of duty, but for the reasons indicated I shall be glad of the views of the Department."

The Secretary replied, August 29th, 1865, among other things : —

"You transmit a list of the articles, contained in the trunks in question, which were determined by the Appraisers to be dutiable, and the value, and rate and amount of duty affixed to each article. Excepting a small piece of carpeting of trifling value, the use of which I do not know, the articles on this list seem to correspond with the declaration made, being ladies' clothing ; and the quantity of them does not seem to me unreasonably large for three ladies, such as you represent these, returning from Europe, with the exception, perhaps, that the quantity of gloves and bonnets may be somewhat larger than usual, though not obviously excessive, if, as I conjecture, the persons you refer to, are among the wealthiest as well as most respectable citizens of Boston.

"You say that friends of this party who are influential citizens, have censured you severely for the course that was taken. You do not state why you have been censured, and I do not understand from your letter upon what points in this case you wish the views of the Department, whether in regard to the quantity of the different articles, or otherwise. Please inform me."

I thought I had made the ground of complaint against me clear, but the Secretary seemed not to understand me, so I wrote him again as follows : —

"The law exempts from duty 'wearing apparel *in actual use*' only. (See Section 2, Art. March 3d, 1857.)   *   *   *   *   *
"The articles returned by the Appraiser were new, and had just been bought, none of them ever having been in use. It was not pretended that

they had been. No doubt they were by law dutiable. Besides the articles so returned, the baggage contained clothing for three ladies and one gentleman. The officer inquired whether the trunks contained any *dutiable articles*, or any thing besides *clothing in use*, and was told that they *did not.*

"The baggage was examined by another officer; and upon finding some of the dutiable articles, the owner then requested, not before, that they might be sent to the Appraisers and examined there.

"None of the dutiable articles were 'mentioned to the Collector,' as required by the Act of 1799.

"The particular point upon which I desire your views is, *Was it the duty of the officers of the Customs to make the examination for the purpose stated, and to detain the trunks so long as might be necessary for that purpose?*"

On the 7th of September the Secretary, in a letter to my successor, Mr. Hamlin, said, —

"I have before me a letter of the late Collector, dated 31st ultimo, in relation to certain baggage of passengers by the Asia.

"It has never been the practice to demand duties upon wearing apparel which passengers may bring with them into this country in reasonable quantities for their own actual use. The term 'wearing apparel in actual use' has not been considered *literally to mean what one wears upon the person,* but wearing apparel for the actual or personal use of the passengers, such as it would be supposed the station in life of the parties in possession would entitle him or her to make actual use of.

"The case mentioned in the late Collector's letter, — the character of the parties seeming to preclude any suspicion of dishonest intentions, — does not seem to require any further action."

Now a word upon this correspondence. I failed utterly to get the Secretary's views upon the only point I particularly asked or desired . them, viz., whether it was the duty of the officers of the Customs to make the examination at all. This, I stated, was the ground of complaint and the cause of censure. It necessarily must have been, for that was all that had then been done ; and, indeed, it was all I ever did except afterwards to request the owners by letter to pay the duties, but they never paid them, nor replied to my letter. They left the case to be managed by Mr. Hooper in Washington. But I did get from the Secretary an extraordinary construction of the law. He says : "Except a small piece of carpeting of little value, *the use of which I do not know* (as if that could make any difference), the articles in this list seem to correspond with the declaration, being ladies' clothing." The written declaration was "clothing for three ladies and one gentleman," and the added verbal declaration was, that the trunks did *not* contain any *dutiable* articles, nor anything besides clothing *in use.* . But when the examining officer had discovered some dutiable articles, the owner then said there was "a considerable quantity of new goods." They had been bought just before sailing for this country. What were they?

	Value.	Duty.
A piece of Carpeting, . . .	$9.45	$5.40
Artificial Flowers, ...	20.00	10.00
Four dozen pair Kid Gloves, : .	34.00	17.00
Seven Silk Bonnets	42.00	25.20
Thirteen Muslin, Silk and Lace Dresses,	355.00	144.25
Four dozen Linen P. Handkerchiefs,	38.40	13.44
Two Silk Cloaks, ...	40.00	14.00
Two Silk Mantillas, . . .	30.00	10.50
	$568.85	$219.79

And yet the Secretary says these "new goods," all dutiable according to the return of the Appraiser, and according to any construction of the law which has ever been given by a predecessor of the Secretary, or any construction which is not a manifest misconstruction, "correspond with the declaration." He adds :· " The quantity does not seem to me unreasonably large for three ladies, such as you represent these returning from Europe, with the exception, perhaps, that the quantity of gloves and bonnets may be somewhat larger than usual, though not obviously excessive, *if*, *as I conjecture*, the persons you refer to, are among the *wealthiest* as well as most respectable citizens of Boston." (I said nothing about wealthy people, and he got this "conjecture" of course, from Mr. Hooper.) This is, to say the least, an unusual reason or rule by which to determine the quantity of *new* articles of clothing and carpeting persons may buy in Paris just before sailing for this country, and enter here without paying duty. The wealthier the persons the more they may buy and bring for *future* use. The Secretary would allow poor people to bring but little. But "*quantity*" has nothing to do with the question. *Any quantity brought into this country as these were, for future use, is an unlawful quantity to admit to free entry*, and this I do not hesitate to say both the Secretary and Mr. Hooper must have known. They certainly ought to have known it. "Wearing apparel in *actual* use," are the words of the law. And there is no difficulty in determining what the legal sense of the words " in actual use " is. The Secretary did not throw any great light upon their meaning when he said they had " not been considered *literally* to mean what was upon the person." Few would have thought so, even if the Secretary had not said that. But they *have* been considered, and by the Department, to mean only such articles " as it shall be satisfactorily shown *had been* in actual use of the person bringing them into the United States." This was the settled construction of the Department until these letters of the Secretary, and it was the true one. But if the Secretary's construction is to be given to the law, so that new articles of clothing, and carpeting, too (if what it is to be used for is not known), may be brought without paying duty, I submit that the poor should be allowed to bring as much as the wealthy ; as much for future use, I mean. Now the wealthy are not allowed to bring more than the poor. Both are allowed to bring without duty *all* the wearing apparel which *had been* or *was* in actual use, and no more. If the wealthy do actually bring more, it is because from their position and wealth they have larger wardrobes *in actual use*. And the General Regulations, if correctly quoted, agree perfectly with the Circular of 1847, viz., " Such as it would be supposed the situation in life of the party in possession would entitle or *require* him or her to make *actual* use of." Actual use of *when?* Certainly not at some indefinite time in the future. The Secretary, in quoting this passage, omitted the word " require." But the passage obviously relates to the quantity which " had been " and was " in actual use," such as it would be supposed the station in life of the party had " required," and not to new articles of merchandise or clothing for use one, two, or five years hence. Persons may bring what their station has entitled or required them to make actual use of. Any other construction would be unreasonable and unjust, and the present law does not admit of any other.

Now apply the law to this case. The persons referred to had been spending some time in Europe. They had the wardrobe "required" for people visiting Europe "conjectured" to be wealthy, and perhaps fashionable. This, though probably large, they had a right to have passed as free baggage. And all this they had *besides* the "new goods." They had seven trunks, one chest, one bag, and one package. Now suppose they had remained in Europe six months longer, would they have bought these new articles when they did because "required" or needed for actual immediate use? The facts justify me in assuming that they would not. Suppose they had been in this country, would they have bought them when they did because in their station in life they would have required so many new articles for actual immediate use? I assume, again, that they would not. The truth undoubtedly is — they would not pretend to the contrary — they bought these new articles because they could buy them better there than here, not for immediate, but for future use. At any rate, they had not needed them before they landed at Boston. Before that time their numerous bonnets, dresses, gloves, handkerchiefs, flowers, &c., which had been in actual use within the meaning of the law, had been all-sufficient. They had a right to bring as many new articles for future use as they pleased, but the law required them to "mention all such articles to the Collector," and pay the duties on them. No sensible lawyer can say otherwise, *as the law is*, and no Secretary but Mr. McCulloch ever did say otherwise, and he is the last man who ought to have said otherwise to me and my officers, who were doing all in our power to carry out his positive and repeated instructions. He ought to have said the examining officers were entirely right, and I think he would if he had not allowed Mr. Hooper to advise him otherwise. *Under other circumstances, can anybody doubt he would have censured me severely, not merely for transgressing the law, but for violating his positive and pointed instructions, if I had allowed these trunks to pass without examination, or had admitted this list of new goods to free entry after examination.*

Suppose his interpretation of the law is carried out, what will be the practical effect? Whenever a passenger arrives with his wearing apparel which "had been" in use, and with new articles, more or less, for future use, several questions will at once arise with the examining officers in deciding upon the new articles. (1.) What is the situation in life of the passenger? It may sometimes be difficult to decide this exactly. But ascertained as near as it can be, the next question will be, How many new goods does that station in life entitle him to have passed without duty? And if the officer should "conjecture" the passenger to be one of the "wealthiest citizens of Boston," a third question will arise, viz.: How many more new goods would it be reasonable, in consideration of his great wealth, to allow him to take free of duty? But, to say nothing of the manifest injustice of favoring the wealthy in this way, how could you establish a uniform rule? From the necessity of the case the question, How much would be reasonable? would have to be decided by the opinion of the officer, and the consequence would be as many different opinions and results as there are different officers. On the whole, I doubt whether it would be any improvement on the rule, as the law has hitherto been interpreted, of allowing free entry to all wearing apparel "in actual use," embracing all that "had been" used, and collecting duty on all the rest, including carpets, whether it was known what they were to be used for or not.

The Secretary closes his letter to Mr. Hamlin by saying that the case mentioned by the late Collector did not seem to require any further action, the character of the parties seeming to preclude any suspicion of dishonest intentions. Of course nothing dishonest was intended. All they proposed or desired was to pass the goods without paying the duties. When they said they had nothing but wearing apparel in use, they had some way of making it all appear right and honest in their own mind. And in this regard these passengers are not distinguished from a great many "respectable and wealthy" people. Some, when successful, instead of thinking they had done anything wrong, even congratulate themselves upon their skill, and perhaps, as the Secretary says, "laugh at the officers behind their backs." To such an extent is the public mind demoralized on this subject, I am quite aware the judgment of many will be that a very meritorious act was done by these passengers, and that Mr. Hooper did entirely right in using the influence he happened to have with the present Secretary, to set the law aside in favor of the "wealthiest as well as the most respectable citizens of Boston." For this is what was done. No further action meant, not even the collection of duty, and it has not been collected. The law provides that if "articles subject to duty shall be found in the baggage of any person arriving in the United States, which shall not at the time of entry be mentioned to the Collector, by the person making the entry, all such articles shall be forfeited, and the person in whose baggage they shall be found, shall moreover forfeit and pay treble the value of such articles." I never asked the forfeiture of the goods, nor the payment of treble in value, but did request, as I have said, a payment of the duty. The parties would have paid the duty in half an hour if Mr. Hooper (whom they will hold responsible for this notice of their case), had advised it. But he preferred to appeal to the Secretary, and never said anything more to me on the subject after the interview I have related at the Custom House. I don't know but he feels proud of his achievement, but it seems to me he must at times feel that this effort, though successful, to save for his friends $219.79 in duties lawfully due the Government, was, after all, rather small business.

THE BORATE CASE.

$12,271.10 Improperly Refunded on Exportation.

A letter from Mr. French, dated at Washington on the 22d of June, 1865, says:—

"I met the Secretary to-day, and after some talk about the recent developments of fraud in Boston, he commented with some prejudice, I thought, on the Borate case, and likened the discipline of the Department to that of a general officer.

"I showed, in brief, how Mr. Fessenden had determined, on a full examination, that you were not to be interfered with, *as on first view he had received an erroneous impression of the case.*"

It seems the Secretary, after I had made every possible effort, without success, to collect a large sum justly and lawfully due the Government as duties, and to prevent a palpable violation of law, and had reluctantly executed the order of the Department·for the third time repeated, to refund the duties on the exportation of 1,363 bags of Borate of Lime, continued to make my conduct in the matter a subject of criticism. How justly, the facts will show. The following is a copy of a letter from the Department : —

"TREASURY DEPARTMENT, July 9th, 1864.
" Sir : — In a letter to you from this Department of May 31st, last, relative to certain Borate of Lime imported into the Port of Boston, Massachusetts, and seized for an alleged violation of the revenue laws, you were instructed, upon a discontinuance of the suit then pending by the District Attorney, to resume your custody of this merchandise, holding it subject to the further orders of this Department.
" You are now instructed to cancel the withdrawal entry for consumption made by Wm. Thwing & Co., if they desire it, and permit them to make an entry for exportation as in other cases, *as said goods have never been removed from the custody or control of the Government.*
" Respectfully, W. P. FESSENDEN,
Secretary of the Treasury.
"J. Z. GOODRICH, Collector, Boston, Mass."

By " exportation as in other cases," was meant with benefit of drawback, or a return of the duties. The order was signed by Mr. Fessenden because he was informed the " goods had never been removed from the custody and control of the Government." Knowing this was a mistake, and that the Secretary had been misinformed, I deemed it my duty to correct him, for the law is, " that no return of duties *shall be allowed* on the export of any merchandise *after it has been removed from the custody of the Government.*" I therefore explained the facts in a letter dated July 13th, as follows : —

" The merchandise was imported and entered for warehousing on the 28th of August, 1862. Two days after, on the 30th, the importers (Wm. Thwing & Co.) paid the duty and made a withdrawal entry for consumption. Whereupon a permit was immediately issued to the Storekeeper directing him to deliver it to them. It appears from the Storekeeper's return, indorsed on the face of the permit, that the goods were ' delivered September 12th, 1862' to Messrs. Thwing & Co. (they did not present the permit till then). On the 11th of October it was ascertained that the duty should have been assessed at 5 cents a pound, amounting to $12,271.10, instead of 20 per cent. ad valorem, amounting to $1,103.40, the sum actually paid, and Messrs. Thwing & Co. were called upon to pay the difference, which they refused to do, claiming that the article was ' mineral ore of Borate,' and subject to 20 per cent. ad valorem. On the 21st of October I proposed to send the General Appraiser and two merchants as experts to examine the article, and report to me what it was, in their opinion. Messrs. Thwing & Co. at first forbid an entry upon the premises, claiming that the importation had been delivered to them on a permit duly obtained at the Custom House, *which was true.* But upon my saying that I should obtain a search warrant to enter their premise, if they persisted in their refusal, they consented. The examination was made, and upon the report of the examiners the property was seized. I only desire to be certain that the facts are understood by the Department."

It would seem hardly possible to imagine a state of facts more conclusively proving that goods had been removed from the custody and control of the Government to the custody and control of the importer and owner, than the foregoing. But it did not satisfy the Assistant Secretaries at the Department.

On the 26th of July, Assistant Secretary Field wrote me acknowledging the receipt of mine of the 13th, and said that Messrs. Thwing & Co. stated that " the merchandise remained where it had been ordered to go on the warehouse entry, in a private *bonded* warehouse, and has never been removed from the same," and desired information from me whether the statement was correct.

To that I replied on the 29th July that " it (the merchandise) was *never* in a *bonded* warehouse, except constructively ; never *actually*, because it remained on board the vessel till it was delivered to Thwing & Co., and on their order it was put into a private warehouse, *private* in every sense, and *bonded* in no sense.

On the 16th of the following August, Assistant Secretary Harrington repeated the instructions to " permit an exportation from warehouse without payment of duty as in other cases of warehoused goods, returning the duty to the importers." He did this on the ground that no bond having been taken for re-delivery " the Government would still have control over the goods *wherever it might find them.*"

A more absurd idea probably never was broached. If that be so, goods in such case can *never* be taken from the custody and control of the Government. These goods, before they were seized, had been in Thwing & Co.'s possession forty days, and feeling sure there must be some mistake or something wrong about it, I still declined to execute the order.

Soon after this Mr. Fessenden, the Secretary, passed through Boston, and I saw him. Upon explaining the case to him it was apparent at once that he had not understood the facts. I told him I was confident exportation could not be allowed with a return of duties, without a plain violation of law, but that I should at once conform to his instructions if I could only be sure he understood the facts. He then asked me to state them to him in a private note, which I did.

On the 16th of September following I received from Assistant Secretary Harrington the following, among other questions, which he desired me to answer, which I did as follows : —

" If, upon the entry, a warehouse permit was given, and if so, was any bonded warehouse designated upon it, and what one?"

" I answer that a warehouse permit was given, upon which ' Kidder's bonded warehouse ' was designated as the place of deposit."

" Was this ' Borate of Lime ' taken to any bonded warehouse in pursuance of the designation on the warehouse permit, and if so, what one? If not taken on a warehouse permit, was it taken without such permit to a bonded warehouse, and if so, to what one?"

" I answer, it was not taken to any bonded warehouse in pursuance of the designation on the warehouse permit, nor was it taken to any bonded warehouse without such permit; in other words, it was never taken to any bonded warehouse."

" Was a bond for re-delivery given as required by the Act of May 28th, 1830, and if not, why not?"

" I answer, that at the time the Borate of Lime was withdrawn, 6,800 bags of ' Nitrate of Soda,' imported by the same parties, at the same time, were also withdrawn. A re-delivery bond, under the act of 28th May, 1830, was taken in a penal sum of double the estimated value of both articles, but in filling up the conditions of the bond, the Borate of Lime was accidentally omitted. Both were delivered to Thwing & Co., direct from the ship, on the permit issued when the duties were paid, and neither ever went into warehouse. The bond expired as soon as the 21st September, certainly, for the examination of the Appraisers was closed on or before the 11th September, as a permit was given on that day to release the two examination packages and deliver them also to Thwing & Co., and they were delivered. The demand for re-delivery under the bond, must have been made, if at all, within ten days from the Appraiser's examination, when the bond expired."

The idea that this Borate of Lime remained in the custody and control of the Government after it passed into the full, undisputed, actual possession of Thwing & Co., simply because it was not inserted in the condition of this bond, is, as I have said, absurd. What had the bond to do with the question of *custody?* and especially could have to do with it after it had expired by its own terms, and was a mere piece of waste paper? For the Borate was in Thwing & Co.'s warehouse at least thirty days after even the examination packages had been delivered, and the bond had expired long before it was seized. But the bond had nothing to do with the question of custody, either before or after it expired. If there had been any occasion to demand a re-delivery of the goods during the ten days before the expiration of the bond, this would have been the consequence. The Government would have had the security of a bond for the re-delivery of the Nitrate of Soda, but no such security for the re-delivery of the Borate of Lime. Not being in the bond, therefore, would seem to make the case, if anything, stronger against the custody of the Government and in favor of that of Thwing & Co. The Government had not even a bond to re-deliver the Borate.

I said further in my letter replying to Mr. Harrington's questions, as follows : —

" In the invoice the article is called 'Crude Borax,' while in the entry Thwing & Co. called it ' Mineral Ore of Borate.' On the trial it was proved to the satisfaction of the jury, who rendered a verdict for forfeiture, that Thwing & Co. knew the article was ' Borate of Lime ' and subject to a duty of 5 cents a pound, but they entered it as ' Mineral ore of Borate,' subject to a duty of 20 per cent. ad valorem.

" The amount of duty paid at 20 per cent. ad valorem was $1,103.40. The amount that should have been paid at 5 cents a pound was $12.271.10. The amount unpaid, viz., $11,167.70, it seems to me to be my duty to institute proceedings to collect."

Such were the facts as I presented them to the Department. A clearer case of fraud has rarely ever been presented to a jury. The evidence was abundant from Thwing & Co.'s own letters. But upon questions of law the case was finally decided in their favor, though the verdict was against them. Under these circumstances I saw no reason why, in violation of a plain and positive provision of law, they should be aided to evade not only the payment of the balance of the duty, but to receive back the amount already paid, and I deemed it my duty to institute proceedings to recover the balance, viz., $11,-167.70, and did so, and obtained security by attaching the property. The duty either on Borate of Lime or Crude Borax was five cents a pound, and there could have been no doubt of recovering that amount.

Some time after I forwarded the facts in a private note to Mr. Fessenden, Mr. Dorrance, the General Appraiser, saw him in Washington. He told Mr. Dorrance that if he had understood the facts he should not have issued the order for exportattion ; that he was satisfied the Collector was right, and should not interfere further, but allow him to proceed and collect the balance of the duty. Mr. Dorrance so reported to me on his return from Washington, and I acted. accordingly. Afterwards I saw Mr. Fessenden himself, and he made the same statement to me. From September to the next March, when he left the Department, I had his approval in the prosecution to recover the balance of the duty, though the order to allow the export and refund the duty had not been formally revoked. It is hardly to be supposed that during all this time the Assistant Secretary had not learned Mr. Fessenden's views.

I heard nothing more till I received the following letter : —

"TREASURY DEPARTMENT, June 6th, 1865.

" Sir : — My attention has been directed by Wm. Thwing & Co. to the fact that the instructions given you on the 9th of July last in regard to the 1,363 bags ' Borate of Lime,' have not been complied with.

" The question submitted in your letter of the 13th of July, 1864, relative to the continued custody of this lime on the part of the Government, having been duly considered, it is my opinion that no *serious violation* would be done to the law or regulations, *by considering this merchandise as having been from the beginning in the custody of the Collector,* and therefore subject to withdrawal.

" You will therefore upon receipt of this, carry into effect the decision of my predecessor of the 9th July, 1864, a copy of which is inclosed. You will also after the ' Borate of Lime ' shall have been exported, return to Wm. Thwing & Co. the money deposited with you as duties thereon; and you will direct the District Attorney to discontinue the suit now pending for additional duties upon this ' Borate of Lime,' upon the payment by them of the costs of said suit.

" Respectfully,   H. McCULLOCH, Secretary of Treasury.
J. Z. GOODRICH, Esq., Collector, Boston."

It is perfectly easy to " consider " things to be true which are not. So it was easy to " consider " this merchandise as having been *from the beginning* IN THE CUSTODY OF THE COLLECTOR, though nothing can be more certain than that it was not. No *serious* violence ! I hardly know what the Secretary means by serious violence to the law. His language implies that he thought the law was violated, but not *seriously.* · When an importer pays the duties on his goods and takes them into his own possession, and means to do it, and the Government means to have him; when he " controls " them by giving directions where to store them on his own premises, and they are stored in accordance with his directions, and the Government means they shall be, as was true in this case, then the custody passes from the Government or Collector to the importer or owner, — the goods are " removed from the custody of the Government " to his " custody " within the meaning of the law. If this is not what the law means, then it is unintelligible. And when this is done the importer's right to a refund of duty upon exportation ceases, and every officer, from the President down, is *prohibited* from allowing it. The goods in James M. Beebe & Co.'s store were no more completely and absolutely taken possession of by them and in their custody, than was this Borate of Lime by Thwing & Co., and it would have been just as lawful to have refunded to Beebe & Co. the duties on every dollar of their merchandise if they had exported it, as it was to refund the $1,103.40 to Thwing & Co. on the exportation of the Borate, or rather the $12,271.11, for it was practically a refund of the whole amount.

When I saw Mr. McCulloch I alluded to this " Borate case," but he refused in a very few words to hear anything on the subject, saying Assistant Secretaries Harrington and Hartley said it was right

I knew the Assistant Secretaries had urged the arguments for exportation and refund, and Mr. Hooper had urged the same views upon me at the Custom House, and at Washington also, I had no doubt. Nevertheless, the balance of the duties should have been collected and paid into the Treasury. Why there should have been the persistent opposition to this course on the part of the Assistant Secretaries, I never could understand. I did all I could to have the collection made, and am willing to take the responsibility of having made the effort. If I erred, it was in finally obeying the order. But when it was repeated the third time, and I knew from the Secretary's reference to my letter of the 13th July, that he understood the facts, I informed him that his predecessor had been satisfied that I was right, and had decided to allow me to collect the balance of the duty, and then, feeling that the responsibility was not on me, I allowed the exportation to be made, and refunded the $1,103.40 of duty already paid.

INTERVIEW WITH THE SECRETARY.

In the interview I had with the Secretary, already referred to, after he had declined to hear any explanation from me in regard to Mr. Dix's removal, I said if agreeable to him I should like to call his attention for a few moments to the subject of my continuance in office, to which, as I understood, it had often been called by others. He at once said, as near as I can repeat his words : — " Probably there will be a change ; there has been no final decision, but that is the expectation. It will be made, however, in a way that will in no manner affect you, as you will all go out together" (meaning Collector, Naval Officer, and Surveyor), adding "*there is nothing in the affair against you.*" He went on to assign the reasons for the proposed change ; said, to use his own words, "it is necessary on party grounds ; the Republican organization cannot be sustained without making changes in offices so lucrative as these." I replied that I should be the last man to complain of a general policy such as he indicated, because in its execution it might reach me, but the difficulty was the Administration had no such policy ; it was all the other way, so far as I knew. I referred to the recent re-appointment of the United States Marshal, District Attorney, and Postmaster of Boston. I know, said Mr. McCulloch, that is as you state, but I would not have re-appointed Mr. Palfrey. But did *you* not, I inquired, only the week before re-appoint Mr. Thomas, of Philadelphia, to the very office in that city which I hold in Boston, and at the same salary? Yes, he replied, that is true, but it was done with no understanding that it was to continue. I do not know, said I, how long it is to continue, I only know that he has just been re-appointed. I was re-appointed on the 13th of March by Mr. Lincoln, and I hold a renewed commission signed by him and yourself. The question therefore is, does the policy of the Administration and the best interest of the Republican organization — for it is on that ground you put it entirely — require Mr. Thomas's *re-appointment* and my *removal?* So far as I know there has not been a single removal among those who had been re-appointed by Mr. Lincoln. The rule has been to re-appoint, rather than to remove those who had been re-appointed. It will, therefore, look like singling out and removing me, not to sustain the Rupublican organization, but for some other reason. This is substantially what passed between us on this point.

If this was the reason for my removal, and there was nothing in the office against me, is it not a little singular that the Secretary was not more frank and communicative on other subjects? It was more than two months after his confidential correspondence with the Messrs. Williams in regard to the rumored missing $32,000, of which I had then heard nothing. If he had any suspicion against me of wrong in that matter, he had no right to tell me there was nothing in the office against me. If he had no such suspicion, why did he not confer with me, as well as with the parties who had paid so much, if not to bribe, at least to improperly influence somebody in the settlement — which is the only inference to be drawn from their own testimony. I was the Collector, and the very officer to confer with, if not suspected. And how came the Messrs. Williams to disclose the fact that they had made any such payment at all? for they must have disclosed it. I had heard of their great desire to procure my removal, and of their willingness to contribute liberally towards it, and it may be safely assumed that such was their desire. They certainly would have kept any such payment to themselves if some strong motive had not impelled them to disclose it. What other motive could have influenced them than the hope that it might in some way be used in accomplishing my removal? Assuming this to have been the motive, — and I can think of no other, — it shows the instrument the Secretary was wittingly or unwittingly using. How they first presented the matter in their correspondence with him, I cannot learn. That is *confidential*. But why should the Secretary treat it as confidential, so far as I was concerned, if there was nothing against me in it? It is known that Mr. Hooper, while talking with other members of the delegation in regard to my removal, said he also had a confidential letter from the Secretary, and that the Department thought there was something wrong about this Williams settlement. This was all before I saw the Secretary, and I inquire again, if he gave the true reason for removing me, and there was no suspicion against me, why did he not say something to me about this matter? If he suspected somebody else and not me, why did he not tell me he proposed to order an investigation before the grand jury? But if he suspected me, why did he not order an investigation before my removal, and notify me, that I might leave the office exonerated, or with the suspicion confirmed? Why was I kept in ignorance, and why, every now and then, were things allowed to come from the Department calculated to excite suspicion against me, if really there was none?

In reply to the Secretary's suggestion that the office was a lucrative one, I said I had made nothing by it during my first term, or during the war. You don't mean, he inquired, that you have not received a large salary and more or less perquisites. No, sir, I answered, but I gave it all beyond enough for my current expenses, which were not extravant, to the support of the war in some form or other, either through the Government direct, or the various voluntary organizations which grew out of the war and were used indirectly as aids and supports to it. Finding myself in office when the war broke out, I determined while it lasted to devote what I made by it to the country in some way, and did. The Secretary responded, "I know it, Mr. Goodrich, I have learned all this from other sources, and have no doubt it is true ; and I know another thing, I know you well enough to know that if you had not been in office, you would have done just as much for the war." I thanked him, and simply remarked that of course I should have had less to do with.

The Secretary did, however, finally say that I was unpopular with the merchants. This I admitted was true with a certain class of merchants, and if that unpopularity was deemed to be a sufficient reason for removal, when the cause of it was considered, I had not a word to say. I could not promise a change that would be at all satisfactory to the merchants referred to. I claimed, however, that it was not true with another class of merchants, importers and citizens, who desired an honest, impartial, and faithful administration of the office. As evidence of this I handed the Secretary papers of which the following are copies, furnished without solicitation on my part, which he read. I avail myself of them now not alone because they were part of the case before the President and Secretary, but especially because an attempt has been made to injure me as a man of integrity : —

" *To the Hon. H. McCulloch, Secretary of the Treasury :*

" Sir : — Will you permit the undersigned, merchants and citizens of Boston, to give expression to our hearty and entire satisfaction with the course of the Hon. John Z. Goodrich, during the four pears of his Collectorship at this port ; and to testify to the ability, impartiality, fidelity, and general public approval with which he has performed the various and difficult duties of his office. If he has not secured the full approval of the entire business community, we cannot but attribute any dissatisfaction which may exist, to the conscientiousness with which he has administered his trust, and to the determination he has continually manifested that the interests of the Government, so far as confided to him, might be always and fully protected and promoted.

" We venture, therefore, to express the earnest hope, that for the sake of the commerce of Boston and the benefit of the revenue service of the United States, it will be in accordance with the views and arrangements of the Department that Mr Goodrich should continue to occupy the position of Collector of Customs at this port, and trust that we may rely on your personal influence to that end. We have the honor to subscribe ourselves,

"Yours very truly,
" Boston, July 3d, 1865.

"J. M. Forbes,	Alpheus Hardy & Co.,
Charles G. Loring,	W. Ropes & Co.,
Edward S. Tobey,	George C. Richardson,
James M. Beebe & Co.,	John M. S. Williams,
James L. Little,	Amos A. Lawrence,
Charles Stoddard,	Samuel H. Walley,
Samuel R. Payson,	Thomas Lamb,
Jabez C. Howe,	Osborn Howes,
C. F. Hovey & Co.,	Jas. H. Beal,
White, Brown & Co.,	F. Haven,
J. Wiley Edmands,	T. P. Chandler,
E. A. Boardman,	Daniel Denny,
Benjamin E. Bates,	E. R. Mudge,
William Claflin,	W. D. Forbes,
Homer Bartlett,	J. C. Tyler & Co."
William Hilton & Co.,	

" Boston, July 18th, 1865.
" Dear Sir : — I hear that there is an attempt being made by parties in this city to remove the Hon. J. Z. Goodrich from the office of Collector of this port. Mr. Goodrich has enjoyed, for a long time, the confidence of the sup-

porters of the Government in the State, and received his appointment on the unanimous recommendation of the Delegation.

"He has always labored earnestly for the success of the Union cause, and contributed most generously of his means for that purpose.

"No one questions his integrity, or his faithfulness and care of the interests of the Government. He has discharged the duties of his office with general acceptance, and the few complaints that are made are from those whose interests have been antagonistic to the Government, and who have felt themselves aggrieved by his care and vigilance.

"His removal at the present time would encourage those who are ready to defraud the revenue, to persist in their peculations, and deter honest and faithful officers from active perseverance in ferreting out corruption and fraud.

"Shall men who have swindled the Government out of hundreds of thousands of dollars, seek to obtain their revenge in this manner?

"I speak plainly, for I believe no good can come by the removal of the present Collector, and that it is mainly sought by those whose sympathies have not been, and are not now with the Government.

"I will add, that I am under no obligation in any way to the Collector, and that I have no interest in the matter other than to have a capable, faithful, honest man, as he has proved himself, in so important a position as the chief of the Boston Custom House.

"I am, sir, with the highest respect, yours truly,
"WILLIAM CLAFLIN,
"Chairman of the Republican Committee.
"To the President."

"WORCESTER, (Mass.), July 10, 1865.

"Sir:—I have been informed that some efforts are likely to be made to procure a change in the office of Collector of the port of Boston.

"I do not know who may be spoken of; but I do know that Mr. Goodrich, who has but recently received a re-appointment, is not only most faithful and able as an officer—fully up to the highest standard of requisite qualifications—but is in full sympathy and confidence with the Republicans of Massachusetts and New England.

"Mr. Goodrich, for the whole term of the existence of the Republican party, has been a generous and laborious friend. He labored in season and out of season as a member of the National Executive Committee, and was regarded, everywhere all over the country, as one of the pillars of that organization. His purse and his time have been given alike to the cause. I cannot see any possible reason why he should be relieved of his office.

"Very respectfully,
"ALEXANDER H. BULLOCK,
"Speaker Mass. House Representatives.
"THE HONORABLE, THE SECRETARY OF THE TREASURY."

The following extract from a letter from J. F. Bailey, Esq., so long Special Agent of the Department, to Secretary McCulloch, dated July 3d, 1865, I did not hand him, but he had received it through the mail:—

"I have known intimately the official character and conduct of Mr. Goodrich, and of all men whom I have so known, there is no one more loyal to public duty, more firm or clear in his political convictions and actions, or more frank and honorable in personal relations. I know of no officer of the Customs service whose conduct has been regulated more completely by the single consideration of duty, than in the case of the present Collector."

No man could have had a better opportunity to form a correct opinion of my official conduct than Mr. Bailey. It was part of his duty, as special agent, to inform himself on that very point.

Let me not be understood as objecting simply because I was removed from office. I never laid the leaving of office to heart a moment, and was glad to be succeeded by so true a man as Mr. Hamlin. In the matter of office holding nobody has rights, — certainly I never claimed any — and consequently no one has a right to complain simply because he has been dismissed from the public service.

I was made Collector — the only office I ever held by appointment under the Government, — upon the unanimous request of the Massachusetts delegation. I did nothing whatever to obtain the office, and when the subject of my removal began to be agitated, I determined to do nothing to retain it. I however afterwards at the earnest and repeated request of a good many friends, consented to take the testimonials which had been voluntarily furnished me, and go to Washington, and present them with my respects to the Secretary, whom I desired to see also on other matters. I told him they represented correctly the general sentiment of Boston and vicinity, as I had been assured and believed, which was all I proposed to say on the subject. What further I said was in reply to statements made by him of his reasons for the removal. I never thought the Secretary was candid in what he said on that subject.

Let me rather be understood as only desiring, besides exposing gross frauds and improprieties, to maintain the integrity of my record as collector against any and all who have attempted to impeach it. If nothing had been done but to remove me, I should have been more than content and never made this exposition and defence. The exposition has sufficiently indicated my conduct and the principles that govern me, to enable every one to decide for himself whether I was right or wrong. That is the question, and the whole of it. Was my course as collector *right* or *wrong?* I have no interest in this question which is separate from the public interest. What I did as collector, I did for the public, and if it was right the public must approve it or lower the standard of honesty and morals. I think the standard should be raised rather than lowered. It is just as dishonest to defraud the Government as to defraud an individual, though many do not so regard it. And there are many ways of defrauding the Government. It may be done, and is often done, by a dishonest interpretation or perversion of the law, and this mode of taking mony from the Treasury is just as fraudulent as any other.

As to my unpopularity of which so much has been said, I hazard nothing in saying that ninety-nine hundredths of it may be accounted for by the cases I have explained, and others like, are not very unlike them, which may be as satisfactory explained, and shall be if necessary. Some of these are still pending, and cannot now be properly explained. But I should like to see the merchant who has been ready to disclose the exact truth, and conform to the requirements of the law, who has had any difficulty with me.

Quite too much stress has been laid on the want of commercial *experience.* How could more *commercial* experience have aided me in dealing with the Williams and Chenery frauds? They were simple and pure frauds, but no more difficult to comprehend because they occurred in commercial transactions. Even *less* of a certain kind of commercial experience would have been of decided advantage in the cases I have related. The truth is, as I intimated at the commencement, the greater want is more commercial *integrity.*

The law has been my guide, and I have believed in giving it the same interpretation to-day that was given to it yesterday, and the same also, whether applicable to our class or another.

The Difference.

My acts under Secretaries Chase and Fessenden were approved, and after a four years' term of service; the lamented Lincoln wrote me and said, "I am not aware of any objection, *personal, political, or official* to your re-appointment." But under Secretary McCulloch and President Johnson, my acts were disapproved, and in some instances Mr. McCulloch reviewed and reversed the decisions of his predecessors.

www.ingramcontent.com/pod-product-compliance
Lightning Source LLC
Chambersburg PA
CBHW030709110426
42739CB00031B/1441